THE PHILOSOPHY
OF EMERSON

THE PHILOSOPHY OF EMERSON

A CONVERSATION BETWEEN RALPH WALDO EMERSON AND ERNEST HOLMES

UPDATED AND GENDER-NEUTRAL

ERNEST HOLMES

newt
LIST

A Newt List Publication
Chicago • New York

CONTENTS

FOREWORD

by Mitch Horowitz

Is there an American spirituality? One with no specific church or rulebook, but that weaves through our religious culture and self-help traditions? I say there is—and it can be found in the pages of this brief, powerful book.

The Philosophy of Emerson exposes us to the intermingled voices of Transcendentalist philosopher Ralph Waldo Emerson (1803-1882) and mystic Ernest Holmes (1887-1960). These two iconic figures gave voice to a single vision: Our minds are endowed by God with creative properties, and what we think determines, literally, what we experience.

This philosophy, sometimes called New Thought, runs through America's vast self-help literature and is found in the hearts of much of the public, who believe, rightly, that the individual can surpass what is said to be factually achievable.

The Philosophy of Emerson does more than highlight the ideas of two great seekers. It shows how all ideas emanate from One Source.

In the past, I have referred to the metaphysics of positivity as "Applied Transcendentalism"—and this book reminds me why. Emerson and Ernest Holmes worked more than a generation apart but came from the same New England climate of spiritual radicalism and experimentation. Entering early adulthood, both thinkers grew convinced that ideas about God and higher laws, if they are authentic, must be instructional and practical. Spiritual insight is self-help, or it is no insight at all.

While still in his early twenties, Ernest, an aspiring writer and philosopher, found in Emerson a thinker who catalyzed his own ideas about the creative properties of the mind. Beginning around 1907, when Ernest turned twenty, he bounced between his childhood home in Lincoln, Maine, and the cultural thoroughfares of Boston, where the youthful seeker absorbed a wide range of spiritual teachings, including the Christian Science theology of Mary Baker Eddy. Although Ernest deeply admired Mrs. Eddy, only in Emerson did he find the simplicity and naturalness of thought that helped him frame and express his own insights. When Ernest began writing about the causative powers of the mind, his tone came from Emerson: Ernest sought to develop not a set of codified strictures but rather an open-ended body of principles on how to live a dynamic and creative existence.

Ernest thrilled to Emerson's core idea, which appears throughout this volume: There is no difference between a mental and spiritual act. The very act of thinking is, in itself, an expression of the Creator. Ernest already had the words to express this; but Emerson put the steel of intellectual confidence into his spine. In Emerson's work, Ernest encountered the same thoughts that he had felt himself; he was astonished to discover within the words of a great, validated, and hallowed philosopher the very things that he had reflected upon while wandering the fields of central Maine.

This kind of self-recognition, this stumbling upon one's most intimately felt truths in the work of another, Emerson taught, is a natural law: All truth across time, if it is enduringly true, is one and the same. Whatever great thing you or I may think today was once thought by Moses, Shakespeare, Lao Tzu, Teresa of Avila. Greatness and truth are not functions of individual genius any more than electricity is a function of conductive wires. We are all channels and receptors; the more receptive we are, the greater the truth that flows through us. As Emerson wrote in History: "There is one mind common to all individuals. Everyone is an inlet to the same and to all of the same." ⋆

This universal over-mind can raise us to extraordinary heights; albeit ones for which we are suited by temperament and training. "When we are in line with spiritual laws," Ernest observed, "we are automatically propelled into right action and easy accomplishment."

Ernest drank in Emerson's insights on worldly achievement: Do not elbow for personal gain, or be clever in money-getting or any other worldly pursuit; rather, be so unencumbered by guile or craftiness as to be set into flight by the patterns and energies of creation, and clothed in the goodness of the natural world like the lilies of the field.

This was the shared vision of Emerson and his soon-to-be influential admirer. It is a vision that, in various forms, traverses today's religious landscape.

Ernest insisted that Science of Mind, as he called his own transcendental philosophy, must be "open at the top"—that is, porous and naturally changeable as nature's laws become more visible to the seeker, and as we learn new methods and techniques to see clearly. Here, too, we find the influence of Emerson. The Yankee sage inveighed against scholasticism and overly

⋆ My quotes reflect the gender-neutrality of the present edition.

complex pedantry. Emerson's work rescued the impressionable young Ernest from formulating a religious doctrine and setting a wall around it. Rather, Emerson emboldened Ernest to create a kind of anti-doctrine: to simply announce the presence of vital, natural laws, and then challenge the readers to test matters for themselves.

As I've noted, both Emerson and Ernest said much about throwing aside your small ambitions so as to merge with the stream of natural laws and be lifted in their currents. None of this, however, means abandoning your sense of individuality. "Everyone has this call of the power to do something unique," Emerson wrote in Spiritual Laws, "and no one has any other call."

We situate ourselves in the flow of spiritual laws when we listen to that call that draws us nearer to what we love, toward what is natural and easy—not "easy" in a frivolous or lazy sense, but in the sense that our personal powers are engaged in effortless play. As Ernest put it: "Each person is an individualized center of God-conscious life and divine action. Each is a unique individualization. When people obey the dictates of the inner voice, they find every pathway open before them."

If this book leaves you with one lesson, let it be from this statement by Emerson: "The soul's emphasis is always right." That exquisitely simple principle guided Ernest on his life journey, and confirmed for him his style of thought and expression. Let it guide you, too.

MITCH HOROWITZ *is a PEN Award-winning historian and the author of* Occult America *and* One Simple Idea, *a history and analysis of New Thought. Visit him at* www.MitchHorowitz.com.

PREFACE

"Reading Emerson was like drinking water to me," Ernest Holmes once said. "I have studied him all my life."

Such endorsement from the creator of the Science of Mind philosophy carries great weight. Not that the work of Emerson has ever required such approbation. Since Emerson began disseminating his ideas through essays and lectures, he has influenced writers, poets, and great thinkers around the world.

In the nineteenth century, Emerson was considered quite radical in his spiritual ideas, believing as he did that all things are divine because everything is connected to God. This caused his detractors to feel that Emerson was removing God from theology as its central figure. Yet as it turned out, nothing could have been further from the truth.

Emerson believed that every human being is an individualization of God, the sole originating force. He believed that each person is operated on by self-executing spiritual laws. It was his belief that God does not necessarily reveal truth, but that truth could be understood by observing nature and the world around us. Though these were radical ideas for nineteenth century minds, it was just this type of independent thinking that attracted a young Ernest Holmes.

When he was merely twenty years old, Holmes inadvertently pick up his brother Fenwicke's copy of *Ralph Waldo Emerson's Essays*. Later, Fenwicke was quoted as saying, "It was at that moment that life really began for Ernest."

"Reading Emerson for the first time," Ernest Holmes said, "the first half-dozen lectures or essays gave me a realization that, in a certain sense, every person has to interpret the universe in terms of their own thinking and personal relationships, and that in order to do it, we have to have faith and confidence in our own interpretation." It is two of these essays, "History" and "Spiritual Laws," that seem to have especially inspired Ernest Holmes.

At some point in his career, Holmes wrote responses to Emerson's essays on History and Spiritual Laws.

It is unclear when he wrote these notes, or whether he wrote them intermittently over several years, but it appears to have been sometime in the 1920s, after penning his landmark book *The Science of Mind*. His notes were later transcribed (where legible) and numbered to correspond with the paragraphs of each Emerson essay, though whether due to faulty transcription of the original handwritten text or mistakes in the manuscript itself, these numbers did not always accurately correspond to the actual Emerson essay. Additionally, the original version of Holmes' notes did not contain the original sections of the essay to which Holmes referred, hindering readers from easily correlating Emerson's text to Holmes' responses.

This first edition of *The Philosophy of Emerson* incorporates the original Emerson passages, followed directly by the corresponding comments of Ernest Holmes, offering itself as a conversation between these two great thinkers, and more strongly illuminating both the influence of Emerson on Holmes and the manner in which Holmes took Emerson's ideas to an original place of personal power.

As Holmes once said, "You are an individualization of God. There is a depth and meaning to your own being. If you can discover it, it will answer your own questions."

RANDALL FRIESEN, *Editor*

SPIRITUAL LAWS

Spiritual Laws

Emerson viewed the universe as both visible and invisible, and as a spiritual system, the material universe being a counterpart of the spiritual. Humankind is a part of the spiritual order, so indivisibly united with it that the entire cosmos is, or may be, reflected in our mind.

Evolution is an awakening of the soul to a recognition of its unity with the whole. Material evolution is an effect, not a cause. This reverses the popular belief, declaring that evolution is the result of intelligence rather than intelligence being the result of evolution. Emerson believed in a spiritual system transparent through the material, in a soul element running through all nature, in a universe governed by law, in a parallel between physical and spiritual laws, and in the interpretation

3

of the spiritual through the physical.

In his essay "Powers and Laws of Thought," in the seventh paragraph, he states: "I believe in the existence of the material world as the expression of the spiritual or the real, and in the impenetrable mystery which hides (and hides to absolute transparency) the mental nature. I await the insight which the advancing knowledge of material laws will furnish."

RALPH WALDO EMERSON: When the act of reflection takes place in the mind, when we look at ourselves in the light of thought, we discover that our life is embosomed in beauty. Behind us, as we go, all things assume pleasing forms, as clouds do far off. Not only things familiar and stale, but even the tragic and terrible, are comely as they take their place in the pictures of memory. The riverbank, the weed at the waterside, the old house, the foolish person, however neglected in the passing, have a grace in the past. Even the corpse that has lain in the chambers has added a solemn ornament to the house. The soul will not know either deformity or pain. If, in the hours of clear reason, we should speak the severest truth, we should say that we had never made a sacrifice. In these hours, the mind seems so great that nothing can be taken from us that seems much. All loss, all pain, is particular; the universe remains to the heart unhurt. Neither vexations nor calamities abate our trust. None have ever stated their griefs as lightly as they might. Allow for exaggeration in the most patient and sorely ridden hack that ever was driven, because it is only the finite that has wrought and suffered; the infinite lies stretched in smiling repose.

5

ERNEST HOLMES: In the opening paragraph of "Spiritual Laws," Emerson says, "When the act of reflection takes place in the mind, when we look at ourselves in the light of thought, we discover that our life is embosomed in beauty." Even the common things of life assume a natural goodness, beauty, and dignity when viewed as a whole. Experiences, like beads, are threaded on the continuity of a perceiving soul. Each fills a natural place. None is too important, none isolated; all are necessary. The mind transcends all its conceptions.

Experiences that seemed perverted, disconnected, and tragic are viewed by the soul as incidents, because "the soul will not know either deformity or pain." The soul itself transcends all experiences, gives the lie to contradictions, bridges every chasm, and finds completion within itself. We are robbed when we conceive of ourselves as being separated from the whole. "All loss, all pain, is particular; the universe remains to the heart unhurt." There is something within us that transcends the hurt. There is an abiding trust at the center of our being, a faith unshaken. Sorrow and grief disappear in the light of this central sun, because " it is only the finite has wrought and suffered; the infinite lies stretched in smiling repose."

This thought is illuminating, revealing as it does Emerson's belief that suffering is a result of ignorance, that the Spirit itself is above suffering and exists in a state

of perpetual tranquility. In no sense is this to be confused with a denial of the objective universe or with the
belief that one must renounce the world if one wishes
to enter into a state of peace. Emerson draws no line
between the physical and the spiritual. His idea is not
division, but unity; not separation, but wholeness; not
God and the individual, but God *in* the individual. God
in everything. From the viewpoint of this large order, he
thought and wrote.

EMERSON: The intellectual life may be kept clean and
healthful if we will live the life of nature and not import
into our mind difficulties which are none of ours. No
one need be perplexed in their speculations. Let them do
and say what strictly belongs to them, and though very
ignorant of books, their nature shall not yield them any
intellectual obstructions and doubts. Our young people
are diseased with the theological problems of original
sin, origin of evil, predestination, and the like. These
never presented a practical difficulty to anyone, never
darkened across anyone's road who did not go out of
their way to seek them. These are the soul's mumps and
measles and whooping-coughs, and those who have not
caught them cannot describe their health or prescribe
the cure. Simple minds will not know these enemies.
It is quite another thing that they should be able to give
account of their faith and expound to another the theory

of their self-union and freedom. This requires rare gifts. Yet, without this self-knowledge, there may be a sylvan strength and integrity in that which they are. "A few strong instincts and a few plain rules" suffice us.

HOLMES: Emerson had an implicit trust in a universe whose integrity he never doubted. He infers that our troubles are borrowed, that theological problems are conjured up from the ignorance of our own consciousness—phantoms that we ourselves create, idols of our own misconceptions, goblins of our own fancy. "A simple mind will not know these enemies." Those who have nature as their priest, whose altar is the sanctuary of their own soul, find a communion simple, direct, and complete, a strength and solidarity "in that which they are."

EMERSON: My will never gave the images in my mind the rank they now take. The regular course of studies, the years of academic and professional education, have not yielded me better facts than some idle books under the bench at the Latin School. What we do not call education is more precious than that which we call so. We form no guess, at the time of receiving a thought, of its comparative value. And education often wastes its effort in attempts to thwart and balk this natural magnetism, which is sure to select what belongs to it.

In like manner, our moral nature is vitiated by any interference of our will. People represent virtue as a

struggle and take to themselves great airs upon their at-
tainments, and the question is everywhere vexed when
a noble nature is commended whether the person is not
better who strives with temptation. But there is no merit
in the matter. Either God is there or God is not there. We
love characters in proportion as they are impulsive and
spontaneous. The less people think or know about their
virtues, the better we like them. Timoleon's victories are
the best victories, which "ran and flowed like Homer's
verses," Plutarch said. When we see a soul whose acts are
all regal, graceful, and pleasant as roses, we must thank
God that such things can be and are, and not turn sourly
on the angel and say, "Crump is a better person with his
grunting resistance to all his native devils."

HOLMES: Viewing the universe as a spiritual system, the Spirit as a unitary wholeness, and the individual
as a part of this natural order, Emerson finds no virtue in
fighting the devil. Goodness is natural and normal. Virtue is not an opposite of evil, but is instinctive righteousness; it need not be analyzed. Like a flower, it blooms on
the tree of life, never comparing itself with the soil from
which it sprang, but keeping its face toward heaven.

EMERSON: Not less conspicuous is the preponderance
of nature over will in all practical life. There is less inten-
tion in history than we ascribe to it. We impute deep-
laid, far-sighted plans to Caesar and Napoleon, but the

9

best of their power was in nature, not in them. People of an extraordinary success, in their honest moments, have always sung, "Not unto us, not unto us." According to the faith of their times, they have built altars to Fortune or to Destiny or to St. Julian. Their success lay in their parallelism to the course of thought that found in them an unobstructed channel, and the wonders of which they were the visible conductors seemed to the eye their deed. Did the wires generate the galvanism? It is even true that there was less in them on which they could reflect than in another, as the virtue of a pipe is to be smooth and hollow. That which externally seemed will and immovableness was willingness and self-annihilation. Could Shakespeare give a theory of Shakespeare? Could ever any of prodigious mathematical genius convey to others any insight into their methods? If they could communicate that secret, it would instantly lose its exaggerated value, blending with the daylight and the vital energy the power to stand and to go.

HOLMES: The purpose of nature is greater than human will. The urge for self-expression emanates directly from nature and accounts for much that we often call "the volitional act of humankind." Therefore, people of great genius have sung, "Not unto us, not unto us." The necessity of the times produces the person. The universal urge flows through the individual genius and, when the channel is unobstructed, produces a Shakespeare. But we can furnish no adequate theory to fit these facts, no method to gain this insight. It forever remains the secret of the spontaneous nature that gives unto all people "the power to stand and go."

EMERSON: The lesson is forcibly taught by these observations, that our life might be much easier and simpler than we make it; that the world might be a happier place than it is; that there is no need of struggles, convulsion, and despairs, of the wringing of the hands and the gnashing of the teeth; that we mis-create our own evils. We interfere with the optimism of nature, because whenever we get this vantage-ground of the past or of a wiser mind in the present, we are able to discern that we are begirt with laws which execute themselves.

The face of external nature teaches the same lesson. Nature will not have us fret and fume. It does not like our benevolence or our learning much better than it likes our frauds and wars. When we come out of the caucus or the bank or the Abolition-convention or the Temperance meeting or the Transcendental club into the fields and woods, it says to us, "So hot? my little one."

HOLMES: "We are begirt with laws which execute themselves." In the light of these laws, we find that our petty differences, our "frauds and wars," our mis-creations that mark a wrong approach to good, and that the sorrow and the "gnashing of the teeth" are results of limited vision. The soul will never find its true place in the natural order of a universe until it blends and unites with this natural order. Trouble is self-imposed; peace forever lies calm and serene at the center.

EMERSON: We are full of mechanical actions. We must needs intermeddle and have things in our own way until the sacrifices and virtues of society are odious. Love should make joy, but our benevolence is unhappy. Our Sunday schools and churches and pauper-societies are yokes to the neck. We pain ourselves to please nobody. There are natural ways of arriving at the same ends at which these aim but do not arrive. Why should all virtue work in one and the same way? Why should all give dollars? It is very inconvenient to us country folk, and we do not think any good will come of it. We have not dollars; merchants have. Let them give them. Farmers will give corn, poets will sing, homemakers will sew, laborers will lend a hand, the children will bring flowers. And why drag this dead weight of a Sunday school over the whole Christendom? It is natural and beautiful that childhood should inquire and maturity should teach, but it is time enough to answer questions when they are asked. Do not shut up the young people against their will in a pew and force the children to ask them questions for an hour against their will.

If we look wider, things are all alike. Laws and letters

and creeds and modes of living seem a travesty of truth. Our society is encumbered by ponderous machinery, which resembles the endless aqueducts which the Romans built over hill and dale, and which are superseded by the discovery of the law that water rises to the level of its source. It is a Chinese wall which any nimble Tartar can leap over. It is a standing army, not so good as a peace. It is a graduated, titled, richly appointed empire, quite superfluous when town-meetings are found to answer just as well.

Let us draw a lesson from nature, which always works by short ways. When the fruit is ripe, it falls. When the fruit is dispatched, the leaf falls. The circuit of the waters is mere falling. The walking of human and all animals is a falling forward. All our manual labor and works of strength, as prying, splitting, digging, rowing, and so forth, are done by dint of continual falling, and the globe, earth, moon, comet, sun, star fall forever and ever.

The simplicity of the universe is very different from the simplicity of a machine. Those who see moral nature out and out, and thoroughly know how knowledge is acquired and character formed, are pedants. The simplicity of nature is not that which may easily be read, but is inexhaustible. The last analysis can no wise be made. We judge of people's wisdom by their hope, knowing that the perception of the inexhaustibleness of nature is an immortal youth. The wild fertility of nature is felt in comparing our rigid names and reputations with our fluid consciousness. We pass in the world for sects and schools, for erudition and piety, and we are all the time jejune babes. One sees very well how Pyrrhonism grew up. Everyone sees that they are that middle point whereof everything may be affirmed and denied with equal reason. One is old, one is young, one is very wise, one is altogether ignorant. One hears and feels what you say of the seraphim and of the tin-peddler. There is no permanent wise person except in the figment of the Stoics. We side with the hero as we read or paint, against the coward and the robber, but we have been ourselves that coward and robber, and shall be again, not in the low circumstance, but in comparison with the grandeurs possible to the soul.

HOLMES: "Love should make joy; but our benevolence is unhappy." Emerson was greatly opposed to the average individual's concept of duty, particularly pertaining to spiritual things. The necessary sacrifices arising from a false sense of duty belie and belittle the magnificence of the Spirit. The spontaneous joy of love finds no true expression through a benevolence that is self-imposed. When we worship from a sense of duty, the altar is profaned. There can be no set rules for the spiritual life. The instinctive urge in the child will find its own logical outlet. Questions need not be answered until they are asked; water reaches its own level by its own weight. That which is inherent in us will express, will find its outlet, if we allow it. "When the fruit is ripe, it falls." Even our mechanical laws are subject to a spiritual order and operate under that universal law that is the government of all things. There is too much resistance to nature, too much fight and struggle, and too little acquiescence. We create vast systems of thought destined to failure because they contradict the natural order.

EMERSON: A little consideration of what takes place around us every day would show us that a higher law than that of our will regulates events; that our painful labors are unnecessary and fruitless; that only in our easy, simple, spontaneous action are we strong, and by contenting ourselves with obedience we become divine. Belief and love—a believing love—will relieve us of a vast load of care. O my friends, God exists. There is a soul at the center of nature and over the will of every person, so that none of us can wrong the universe. It has so infused its strong enchantment into nature that we prosper when we accept its advice, and when we struggle to wound its creatures, our hands are glued to our sides, or they beat our own breasts. The whole course of things goes to teach us faith. We need only obey. There is guidance for each of us, and by lowly listening we shall hear the right word. Why need you choose so painfully your place and occupation and associates and modes of action and of entertainment? Certainly there is a possible right for you that precludes the need of balance and willful election. For you, there is a reality, a fit place and congenial duties. Place yourself in the middle of the stream of power and wisdom which animates all whom it floats, and you are without effort impelled to truth, to right and a perfect contentment. Then you put all gainsayers in the wrong. Then you are the world, the measure of right, of truth, of beauty. If we will not be mar-plots with our miserable interferences, the work, the society, letters, arts, science, religion of humans would go on far better than now, and the heaven predicted from the beginning of the world and still predicted from the bottom of the heart would organize itself, as do now the rose and the air and the sun.

I say, do not choose. But that is a figure of speech by which I would distinguish what is commonly called choice among people and which is a partial act, the choice of the hands, of the eyes, of the appetites, and not a whole act of the person. But that which I call right or goodness is the choice of my constitution, and that which I call heaven and inwardly aspire after is the state or circumstance desirable to my constitution, and the action which I in all my years tend to do is the work for my faculties. We must hold people amenable to reason for the choice of their daily craft or profession. It is not an excuse any longer for their deeds, that they are the custom of their trade. What business have they with an evil trade? Have they not a calling in their character?

HOLMES: The individual does not live by will, but by a higher law that controls everything. "Belief and love" are the mainsprings of existence and "relieve us of a vast load of care." "There is a soul at center of nature and over the will of every person, so that none of us can wrong the universe." When we are in line with spiritual laws, we are automatically propelled into right action and easy accomplishment. When, in our ignorance, we oppose these laws, they automatically react against us. Thus, through the misconceptions of our ignorance, we find the return circuits of the law imposing the hardship upon us which we have set in motion toward another. Living by faith and "by lowly listening," our lives are carried on with the stream of existence, freed from pain. Heaven organizes itself in us, and we live naturally as the rose, breathing the pure air of Spirit, living in the light of that eternal sun which is forever ascending, forever radiating from that universal Soul whose center is everywhere.

EMERSON: All people have their own vocation. The talent is the call. There is one direction in which all space is open to them. They have faculties silently inviting them thither to endless exertion. They are like ships in a river; they run against obstructions on every side but one. On that side, all obstruction is taken away, and they sweep serenely over a deepening channel into an infinite sea. This talent and this call depend on their organization, or the mode in which the general soul incarnates itself in them. They incline to do something which is easy to them, and good when it is done, but which no other person can do. They have no rival. For the more truly they consult their own powers, the more difference will their work exhibit from the work of any other. Their ambition is exactly proportioned to their powers. The height of the pinnacle is determined by the breadth of the base. Everyone has this call of the power to do something unique, and no one has any other call. The pretence that any have another call, a summons by name and personal election and outward "signs that mark them extraordinary, and not in the roll of common people," is fanaticism and betrays obtuseness to perceive that there is one mind in all individuals, and no respect of persons therein.

HOLMES: The incarnation of the universal in the individual is the mainspring of Emerson's thought. Each person is an individualized center of God-conscious life and divine action. Each is a unique individualization. When people obey the dictates of the inner voice, they find every pathway open before them. "They have no rival." The "general soul incarnates itself in them."

Through them, the unity of this general soul passes into unique variations of itself. No two people are alike. The more we study our own individuality and seek to build a superstructure on the foundations of our own thought and endeavor, the more power we have. "The height of the pinnacle is determined by the breadth of the base." To believe that anything less than this divine calling is worthy is to fall under the illusion of a separation from the whole and to deny the realization "that there is one mind in all individuals."

EMERSON: By doing their work, these individuals make the need felt which they can supply and create the taste by which they are enjoyed. By doing their own work, they unfold themselves. It is the vice of our public speaking that it has not abandonment. Somewhere, not only every orator, but every person should let out all the length of all the reins; should find or make a frank and hearty expression of what force and meaning is in them. The common experience is that these people fit themselves as well as they can to the customary details of that work or trade they fall into and tend it as a dog turns a spit. Then are they a part of the machine they move; the person is lost. Until they can manage to communicate themselves to others in their full stature and proportion, they do not yet find their vocation. They must find in that an outlet for their character, so that they may justify their work to their eyes. If the labor is mean, let them by their thinking and character make it liberal. Whatever they know and think, whatever in their apprehension is worth doing, that let them communicate, or others will never know and honor them aright. Foolish, whenever you take the meanness and formality of that thing you do, instead of converting it into the obedient spiracle of your character and aims.

HOLMES: When people follow the genius of their own individuality, "they create the taste by which they are enjoyed. They provoke the wants to which they can minister." This is another way of saying that cause and effect are merely two ends of the same thing, and that both cause and effect are spiritual; one follows the other as the night the day. We are ourselves. We give expression to the Universal Mind and do our best work when we give complete attention and enthusiasm to our endeavor, when we are able to "let out all the links of all the reins." Anything less than this stultifies the mind, stunts the effort, inhibits the Spirit, and limits the person. Self-expression is the keynote of life. We exist for the purpose of providing an extension of consciousness through which the universal may work.

EMERSON: We like only such actions as have already long had the praise of others, and do not perceive that anything humans can do may be divinely done. We think greatness entailed or organized in some places or duties, in certain offices or occasions, and do not see that Paganini can extract rapture from a catgut, and Eulenstein from a jews-harp, and a nimble-fingered lad out of shreds of paper with his scissors, and Landseer out of swine, and the hero out of the pitiful habitation and company in which he or she was hidden. What we call obscure condition or vulgar society is that condition and society whose poetry is not yet written, but which you shall presently make as enviable and renowned as any. In our estimates, let us take a lesson from sovereigns. The parts of hospitality, the connection of families, the impressiveness of death, and a thousand other things, royalty makes its own estimate of, and a royal mind will. To make habitually a new estimate, that is elevation.

What individuals do, that they have. What have they to do with hope or fear? In each of us is our might. Let us regard no good as solid but that which is in our nature and which must grow out of us as long as we exist. The goods of fortune may come and go like summer leaves. Let us scatter them on every wind as the momentary signs of their infinite productiveness.

All may have their own. Their genius, the quality that differences them from every other, the susceptibility to one class of influences, the selection of what is fit for them, the rejection of what is unfit, determines for them the character of the universe. Individuals are methods, progressive arrangements, selecting principles, gathering their like to them wherever they go. They take only their own out of the multiplicity that sweeps and circles round them. They are like one of those booms which are set out from the shore on rivers to catch driftwood, or like the loadstone amongst splinters of steel. Those facts, words, persons, which dwell in their memory without their being able to say why, remain because they have a relation to them not less real for being as yet unapprehended. They are symbols of value to those people, as they can interpret parts of their consciousness which they would vainly seek words for in the conventional images of books and other minds. What attracts my attention shall have it, as I will go to the person who knocks at my door, whilst a thousand persons as worthy go by it to whom I give no regard. It is enough that these particulars speak to me. A few anecdotes, a few traits of character, manners, face, a few incidents, have an emphasis in your memory out of all proportion to their apparent significance if you measure them by the ordinary standards. They relate to your gift. Let them have their weight, and do not reject them and cast about for illustration and facts more usual in literature. What your heart thinks great is great. The soul's emphasis is always right.

HOLMES: "Accept your genius and say what you think." Take yourself for better or for worse. Rely on that inner impulse, that intuitive perception, that spiritual genius which lights everyone's path to the gateway of good. Find the divine in the most commonplace things of life. Elevate the human with a positive faith. Trust the integrity of your own soul. Fan the human spark into a blaze divine, and "perceive that anything a person can do may be divinely done."

Do away with the illusion of hope and the morbidity of fear. Realize that no good can be solid unless it is an extension of the self. Play with the gifts of life, "and scatter them on every wind." The gates of the eternal reservoir are forever open, and the "infinite productiveness" knows no drought. The supply is always equal to the demand. People are always united with the Divine, and, searching deeply into their own nature, they find that "in themselves is their might." The mind is a magnet, "a selecting principle, gathering our like to us wherever we go." The natural affinity of the soul irresistibility draws that which belongs to it. The power compelling this movement is an impulse of the Spirit acting in accord with immutable law. Not by conscious choice, but by divine necessity, we gather our own.

EMERSON: Over all things that are agreeable to human nature and genius, the individual has the highest right. Everywhere we may take what belongs to our spiritual estate. We cannot take anything else, though all doors were open, nor can all the force of people hinder us from taking so much. It is vain to attempt to keep a secret from one who has a right to know it. It will tell itself. That mood into which friends can bring us is their dominion over us. To the thoughts of that state of mind, we have a right. All the secrets of that state of mind, we can compel. This is a law which states people use in practice. All the terrors of the French Republic, which held Austria in awe, were unable to command its diplomacy. But Napoleon sent to Vienna M. de Narbonne, one of the old noblesse, with the morals, manners, and name of that interest, saying that it was indispensable to send to the old aristocracy of Europe people of the same connection, which in fact constitutes a sort of free-masonry. M. de Narbonne in less than a fortnight penetrated all the secrets of the imperial cabinet.

Nothing seems so easy as to speak and to be understood. Yet individuals may come to find that the strongest of defenses and of ties, that they have been understood, and those who have received an opinion may come to find it the most inconvenient of bonds.

If teachers have any opinion which they wish to conceal, their pupils will become as fully indoctrinated into that as into any which the teaches publish. If you pour water into a vessel twisted into coils and angles, it is vain to say, "I will pour it only into this or that; it will find its level in all." Individuals feel and act the consequences of their doctrine without being able to show how they follow. Show us an arc of the curve, and a good mathematician will find out the whole figure. We are always reasoning from the seen to the unseen. Hence, the perfect intelligence that subsists between wise people of remote ages. Individuals cannot bury their meanings so deep in their books but time and like-minded people will find them. Plato had a secret doctrine, had he? What secret can he conceal from the eyes of Bacon? of Montaigne? of Kant? Therefore, Aristotle said of his works, "They are published and not published."

HOLMES: There is a "perfect intelligence that subsists between the wise of remote ages." There is a timelessness in the Universal Mind which includes all epochs. When "like-minded individuals" think, disregarding the age in which they live, they tap the same universal stream of consciousness, read the same meaning, discover the same laws, imbibe the same spirit, and proclaim the same truth, each in their own tongue. Thought passes through the individual stream of consciousness back into the universal, to be reinterpreted by other individuals who grasp its meaning. Thus individuals universalize themselves, and thus the Universal individualizes itself.

EMERSON: No one can learn what they have not preparation for learning, however near to their eyes is the object. Chemists may tell their most precious secrets to a carpenter, and the carpenter shall be never be the wiser; the secrets the carpenter would not utter to a chemist for an estate. God screens us evermore from premature ideas. Our eyes are holden that we cannot see things that stare us in the face until the hour arrives when the mind is ripened. Then we behold them, and the time when we saw them not is like a dream.

HOLMES: Since there are no secrets withheld from the Universal Mind, and since all individuals may tap this Mind at a level of their own consciousness, it follows that apparent secrets are merely things with which we have no affinity. Once the affinity is gained, the secret is proclaimed. But, "no one can learn what they have not preparation for learning, however near to their eyes is the object." We are living in eternity now. We are surrounded by a limitless intelligence this moment, and the potential possibilities of the Infinite are already incarnated in us. Not until we are ready will the divine secret be disclosed. When our eyes are opened, we will see. "God screams us ever more from premature ideas." The good we desire will be ours when we are ready for it, when we unite our individual good with that universal good which includes all. We awake from the dream of isolation and separation to discover that we have never been really apart from our good. We have only failed to perceive it.

EMERSON: Not in nature, but in the individual, is all the beauty and worth the individual sees. The world is very empty and is indebted to this gilding, exalting soul for all its pride. "Earth fills its lap with splendors" not its own. The vale of Tempe, Tivoli and Rome are earth and water, rocks and sky. There are as good earth and water in a thousand places, yet how unaffecting!

People are not the better for the sun and moon, the horizon and the trees, as it is not observed that the keepers of Roman galleries or the valets of painters have any elevation of thought, or that librarians are wiser than others. There are graces in the demeanor of a polished and noble person, which are lost upon the eye of a churl. These are like the stars whose light has not yet reached us.

HOLMES: "Not in nature, but in the individual, is all the beauty and worth the individual sees." Nature, without anyone to experience its beauty, remains empty. The pride of creation, on this planet at least, is the consciousness of that being who beholds its splendors. Nor can location or environment make the person. Those places which humans hallow with their presence are sacred not because of the concrete and material fact, but because we weave into the fact a design that our imagery brings to it—a pattern spun from an inner, creative source, the incarnation of the Almighty in the human. Noble people carry with them the light of the stars and all the gifts of heaven. The veil of the temple is rent when we are prepared to enter the Holy of Holies, no matter where the place may be.

EMERSON: One may see what one makes. Our dreams are the sequel of our waking knowledge. The visions of the night bear some proportion to the visions of the day. Hideous dreams are exaggerations of the sins of the day. We see our evil affections embodied in bad physiognomies. On the Alps, travelers sometimes behold their own shadow magnified to a giant, so that every gesture of their hand is terrific. "My children," said an old man to his children scared by a figure in the dark entry, "My children, you will never see any thing worse than yourselves." As in dreams, so in the scarcely less fluid events of the world, all people see themselves in colossal, without knowing that it is themselves. The good, compared to the evil which they see, is as their own good to their own evil. Every quality of their mind is magnified in some one acquaintance, and every emotion of their heart in some one. They are like a quincunx of trees, which counts five, east, west, north or south, or an initial, medial, and terminal acrostic. And why not? They cleave to one person and avoid another, according to their likeness or unlikeness to themselves, truly seeking themselves in their associates, and moreover in their trade and habits and gesture, and meats and drinks, and come at last to be faithfully represented by every view they take of their circumstances.

HOLMES: "One may see what one makes." Each of us lives in a world of our own making. To the pure, all is pure. Evil beholds the image of its own false creation. Emerson instinctively foreknew certain psychological facts that are now common knowledge and anticipated our present theory of dream psychology. "Our dreams are the sequel of our waking knowledge." The peaceful mind, trusting in the universe and believing in the eternal goodness, is calm in the midst of confusion and finds perfect rest in sleep, but the mind distraught by the events of the day, fearful of the future, morbidly introspecting the past, or the mind distraught and evil in its imagination, finds no repose and is continuously tormented by itself.

Asleep or awake, we will never see anything more fearful or more lovely than our own imagination pictures it. Our concept of life is, in imagination, an outline of our introspections. "The good which they see, compared to the evil which they see, is as their own good to their own evil." Emerson never departs from this thought: Each individual is the center of their own universe. Any apparent circumference is a true radiation of this center. As we think, will, and propose, so are we. We are free agents in a universe that denies us nothing, but which reflects back to us an exact representation of our own beliefs.

Emerson's exultation of the individual in no way denies his dependence on the universe, because he con-
tinually reiterates the thought that individuals live by
virtue of their relationship to that universal wholeness
which is incarnated in all.

EMERSON: One may read what one writes. What can
one see or acquire but what one is? You have observed
a skillful person reading Virgil. Well, that author is a
thousand books to a thousand persons. Take the book
into your two hands and read your eyes out; you will
never find what I find. If any ingenious readers would
have a monopoly of the wisdom or delight they get, they
are as secure now the book is Englished as if it were im-
prisoned in the Pelews' tongue. It is with a good book as
it is with good company. Introduce base people among
high society; it is all to no purpose. They are not their
community. Every society protects itself. The company
is perfectly safe, and those people are not one of them,
though their bodies are in the room.

HOLMES: "One may read what one writes." The
revelation of another person is, to us, only the nature
of our own thought. We must bring to the author that
which we expect to take away. The depth which the
author's thought reaches finds an equal deep in our own
minds and reveals us to ourselves. Hence, any author
"is a thousand books to a thousand persons." The great

thinkers of the ages are equally sought by the few who can understand them.

We are all universal. There is a place in each which has the possibility of responding to the most divine concepts. Deep truths remain hidden until the mind is ready to receive them. We draw from each other that which we are. "Every society protects itself." The presence of our physical bodies in any company is no guarantee of an affinity of mind. It is the affinity of mind and Spirit which attracts, compels, and binds.

EMERSON: What avails it to fight with the eternal laws of mind, which adjust the relation of all persons to each other by the mathematical measure of their havings and beings? Gertrude is enamored of Guy; how high, how aristocratic, how Roman his mien and manners! to live with him were life indeed, and no purchase is too great; and heaven and earth are moved to that end. Well, Gertrude has Guy, but what now avails how high, how aristocratic, how Roman his mien and manners, if his heart and aims are in the senate, in the theatre, and in the billiard-room, and she has no aims, no conversation that can enchant her graceful lord?

He shall have his own society. We can love nothing but nature. The most wonderful talents, the most meritorious exertions really avail very little with us. But nearness or likeness of nature, how beautiful is the ease

31

of its victory! People approach us famous for their beauty, for their accomplishments, worthy of all wonder for their charms and gifts. They dedicate their whole skill to the hour and the company, with very imperfect result. To be sure, it would be ungrateful in us not to praise them loudly. Then, when all is done, a person of related mind, a sibling by nature, comes to us so softly and easily, so nearly and intimately, as if it were the blood in our proper veins, that we feel as if someone was gone instead of another having come. We are utterly relieved and refreshed. It is a sort of joyful solitude. We foolishly think in our days of sin that we must court friends by compliance to the customs of society, to its dress, its breeding, and its estimates. But only that soul can be my friend which I encounter on the line of my own march, that soul to which I do not decline and which does not decline to me, but, native of the same celestial latitude, repeats in its own all my experience. Scholars forget themselves and ape the customs and costumes of the person of the world, to deserve the smile of beauty, and follows some giddy child not yet taught by religious passion to know the noble being with all that is serene, oracular, and beautiful in its soul. Let them be great, and love shall follow them. Nothing is more deeply punished than the neglect of the affinities by which alone society should be formed, and the insane levity of choosing associates by others' eyes.

HOLMES: "What avails it to fight with the eternal laws of mind, which adjust the relation of all people to each other, by mathematical measure of their havings and beings?" The laws of mind are mathematical measurers. Unnatural relationships exist only by false coercion. Ultimately, the soul readjusts false relationships and draws its own to it. "They shall have their own society." "How beautiful is the ease of its victory!" When a person whose mind is related to us, "a sibling by nature," comes into the atmosphere of our consciousness, the union is complete. This circulation of consciousness now binds the two into one "so softly and easily, so nearly and intimately, as if it were the blood in our own proper veins," because the eternal laws of mind fulfill their purposes. Thus, the inevitable law of attraction, which the individual cannot resist, accomplishes its end. Thus, the self is forever wedded to the self.

We are attracted to those who meet us on the level of our own evolution, "on the line of my own march." Those whose consciousness appreciates and understands the gods find themselves in their company, while a gross mind still wallows in the mire from which an instinctive urge seeks to extricate it. Companionship and society reflect the soul. When we meet the great through due appreciation and affinity of soul, we meet them not as aspirants, not as candidates unto greatness, but because we too are "native of the same celestial latitude."

A subtle meaning is written in the closing lines of this paragraph, referring to the punishment that follows "the neglect of the affinities by which alone society should be formed." An evil person finds no enjoyment in the company of natural goodness. We find no comfort outside ourselves and those conditions and people who the affinity of our souls draws into the atmosphere of our experiences. Though we were in hell and our minds dwelt on heavenly things, we should immediately find ourselves in heaven. Though we were in heaven and our mind dwelt on evil, we should immediately find ourselves in hell. "Let them be great, and love shall follow them."

EMERSON: They may set their own rate. It is a maxim worthy of all acceptation, that anyone may have that allowance they take. Take the place and attitude which belong to you, and all people acquiesce. The world must be just. It leaves everyone, with profound unconcern, to set their own rate. Hero or driveller, it meddles not in the matter. It will certainly accept your own measure of your doing and being whether you sneak about and deny your own name or whether you see your work produced to the concave sphere of the heavens, one with the revolution of the stars.

The same reality pervades all teaching. Individuals may teach by doing, and not otherwise. If they can communicate themselves, they can teach, but not by words.

Those teach who give, and those learn who receive. There is no teaching until the pupils are brought into the same state or principle in which you are. A transfusion takes place. They are you and you are them. Then is a teaching, and by no unfriendly chance or bad company can they ever quite lose the benefit. But your propositions run out of one ear as they ran in at the other. We see it advertised that one person will deliver an oration on the Fourth of July, and another before the Mechanics' Association, and we do not go thither, because we know that these people will not communicate their own character and experience to the company. If we had reason to expect such a confidence, we should go through all inconvenience and opposition. The sick would be carried in litters. But a public oration is an escapade, a noncommittal, an apology, a gag, and not a communication, not a speech, not a person.

A like nemesis presides over all intellectual works. We have yet to learn that the thing uttered in words is not therefore affirmed. It must affirm itself, or no forms of logic or of oath can give it evidence. The sentence must also contain its own apology for being spoken.

HOLMES: "They may set their own rate." "They may have that allowance they take." Emerson is not speaking of external possessions, but of inner gifts. The world is not at all concerned over us, but leaves us sternly alone to work out our own salvation. Ultimately, we are accepted at our own valuation, provided these values are true and not false ones.

The measurer of our own worth is measured back to us. The measurer is not a person, but "the eternal laws of mind." "Those teach who give, and those learn who receive." There is no teaching unless the teachers have the ability to impart themselves. Seldom do we find people who have overcome the objective barriers and who directly impart themselves. Such will always have an audience, no matter what the topic of their discourse. Anything less than the surrender of the soul is "an apology, a gag, and not communication, not a speech, not a person." The discourse carries with it a conviction equal to the depth of the one giving it, equal to the emotion behind it. Without argument, it finds acquiescence. Almost without words, it bridges the gulf between individual minds.

The inner feeling from which the spoken word is propelled strikes a debt that no rhetoric can measure. The orator is the oration; the speech is the speaker; the sermon is the preacher. Without the artist, there can be no more. A complete surrender of the intellect to the inner genius makes possible the subtle soul communion, strikes fire from heaven, and kindles like a flame in the imagination of other people.

EMERSON: The effect of any writing on the public mind is mathematically measurable by its depth of thought. How much water does it draw? If it awakens you to think, if it lifts you from your feet with the great voice of eloquence, then the effect is to be wide, slow, permanent, over the minds of humans. If the pages instruct you not, they will die like flies in the hour. The way to speak and write what shall not go out of fashion is to speak and write sincerely. The argument which has not power to reach my own practice, I may well doubt, will fail to reach yours. But take Sidney's maxim: "Look in thy heart, and write." They that write to themselves write to an eternal public. That statement only is fit to be made public which you have come at in attempting to satisfy your own curiosity. Writers who take their subject from their ear and not from their heart should know that they have lost as much as they seem to have gained, and when the empty book has gathered all its praise and half the people say, "What poetry! What genius!" it still needs fuel to make fire. That only profits which is profitable. Life alone can impart life, and though we should burst, we can only be valued as we make ourselves valuable. There is no luck in literary reputation. They who make up the final verdict upon every book are not the partial and noisy readers of the hour when it appears, but a court as of angels, a public not to be bribed, not to be entreated, and not to be overawed, deciding upon everyone's title to fame. Only those books come down which deserve to last. Gilt edges, vellum, and morocco, and presentation-copies to all the libraries will not preserve a book in circulation beyond its intrinsic date. It must go with all Walpole's Noble and Royal Authors to its fate. Blackmore, Kotzebue, or Pollok may endure for a night, but Moses and Homer stand forever. There are not in the world at any one time more than a dozen people who read and understand Plato; never enough to pay for an edition of his works. Yet to every generation these come duly down for the sake of those few persons, as if God brought them in God's hand. "No book," said Bentley, "was ever written down by any but itself." The permanence of all books is fixed by no effort friendly or hostile, but by their own specific gravity, or the intrinsic importance of their contents to the constant mind of humankind. "Do not trouble yourself too much about the light on your statue," said Michelangelo to the young sculptor. "The light of the public square will test its value."

HOLMES: "The effect of any writing on the public mind is mathematically measurable by its depth of thought. How much water does it draw?" Authors, to cause us to think, live in our minds. They awaken in us the same concepts, the same emotions and hopes that they themselves have experienced. Those who write from the sincerity of their own souls, who write an answer to the deep questionings of their own minds, are answering the questions of other people's minds, because "there is one mind come into all individual people."

There can be no mistake and no chance in "the final verdict upon every book." Those books come down to us which deserve to live. They are brought by a law of natural affinity and placed in the hands of those ready to receive them, "as if God brought them in God's hand."

EMERSON: In like manner, the effect of every action is measured by the depth of the sentiment from which it proceeds. The great knew not that they were great. It took a century or two for that fact to appear. What they did, they did because they must. It was the most natural thing in the world and grew out of the circumstances of the moment. But now, everything they did, even to the lifting of their finger or the eating of bread, looks large, all-related, and is called an institution.

HOLMES: "The great knew not that they were great." Greatness, like virtue, is natural and flows from the spontaneous mind without effort. Honesty and sincerity are not warriors pitted against crime and ignorance, but are lights shining in the darkness. As the light knows naught of darkness, so virtue knows no vice. Greatness cannot contemplate meanness. The purer soul radiates purity. Good cannot understand evil, while beauty sheds its radiance on ugliness and is unaware of any seeming opposite. People who have towered above the average, whose spirits have been exalted above the commonplace, whose inner awareness has given them a heavenly companionship, have been simple and direct both in speech and in manner. They have done what they did because they must, not even by choice, but through the spontaneous acclamation of their own natures. They may have been egoists, but never egotists. Our institutions are founded upon the thought of these minds.

EMERSON: These are the demonstrations in a few particulars of the genius of nature. They show the direction of the stream. But the stream is blood; every drop is alive. Truth has not single victories. All things are its organs, not only dust and stones, but errors and lies. The laws of disease, physicians say, are as beautiful as the laws of health. Our philosophy is affirmative and readily accepts the testimony of negative facts, as every shadow points to the sun. By a divine necessity, every fact in nature is constrained to offer its testimony.

HOLMES: "Truth has not single victories. All things are its organs." Behind the infinite variations of nature, there is a unitary cause. Even a lie announces our ability to speak. Disease is not an evil of itself, but in its own nature is perfect. There is only one substance from which all things are formed. This substance is always unavailable, always ready to spring into form.

EMERSON: Human character evermore publishes itself. The most fugitive deed and word, the mere air of doing a thing, every intimated purpose expresses character. If you act, you show character. If you sit still, if you sleep, you show it. You think because you have spoken nothing when others spoke and have given no opinion on the times, on the church, on slavery, on marriage, on socialism, on secret societies, on the college, on parties and people, that your verdict is still expected with curiosity as a reserved wisdom. Far otherwise. Your silence answers very loud. You have no oracle to utter, and your neighbors have learned that you cannot help them, because oracles speak. Doth not wisdom cry and understanding put forth its voice?

Dreadful limits are set in nature to the powers of dissimulation. Truth tyrannizes over the unwilling members of the body. Faces never lie, it is said. No one need be deceived who will study the changes of expression. When anyone speaks the truth in the spirit of truth, their eye is as clear as the heavens. When they have base ends and speak falsely, the eye is muddy and sometimes asquint.

I have heard experienced counselors say that they never feared the effect upon a jury of lawyers who do not believe in their heart that their client ought to have a verdict. If they do not believe it, their unbelief will appear to the jury despite all their protestations and will become their unbelief. This is that law whereby a work of art of whatever kind sets us in the same state of mind wherein the artist was when making it. That which we do not believe, we cannot adequately say, though we may repeat the words ever so often. It was this conviction which Swedenborg expressed when he described a group of people in the spiritual world endeavoring in vain to articulate a proposition that they did not believe. But they could not, though they twisted and folded their lips even to indignation.

Individuals pass for that they are worth. Very idle is all curiosity concerning other people's estimate of us, and all fear of remaining unknown is not less so. If we know that we can do anything, that we can do it better than anyone else, we have a pledge of the acknowledgment of that fact by all people. The world is full of judgment days, and into every assembly that anyone enters, in every action they attempt, they are gauged and stamped. In every troop of children that whoop and run in each yard and square, newcomers are as well and accurately weighed in the course of a few days and stamped with their right number, as if they had undergone a formal trial of their strength, speed, and temper. Strangers come from distant schools with better dress, with trinkets in their pockets, with airs and pretensions. The established ones say to themselves, "It's of no use. We shall find them out tomorrow." "What have they done?' is the divine question which searches people and transpierces every false reputation. Fops may sit in any chair of the world, nor be distinguished for their hour from Homer and Washington, but there need never be any doubt concerning the respective ability of human beings. Pretension may sit still, but cannot act. Pretension never feigned an act of real greatness. Pretension never wrote an *Iliad*, nor drove back Xerxes, nor christianized the world, nor abolished slavery.

As much virtue as there is, so much appears. As much goodness as there is, so much reverence it commands. All the devils respect virtue. The high, the generous, the self-devoted sect will always instruct and command humankind. Never was a sincere word utterly lost. Never a magnanimity fell to the ground but there is some heart to greet and accept it unexpectedly. People pass for that they are worth. What they are engraves itself on their faces, on their forms, on their fortunes, in letters of light. Concealment avails them nothing; boasting, nothing. There is confession in the glances of their eyes, in their smiles, in salutations and the grasp of hands. Their sin bedaubs them, mars all their good impression. Others know not why they do not trust them, but they do not trust them. Their vice glasses their eyes, cuts lines of mean expression in their cheeks, pinches the nose, sets the mark of the beast on the back of the head, and writes, O fool! fool! on the forehead of a sovereign.

If you would not be known to do anything, never do it. A person may play the fool in the drifts of a desert, but every grain of sand shall seem to see. Some may be solitary eaters, but they cannot keep their foolish counsel. A broken complexion, a swinish look, ungenerous acts, and the want of due knowledge all blab. Can a cook, a Chiffinch, an Iachimo be mistaken for Zeno or Paul? Confucius exclaimed, "How can a person be concealed! How can a person be concealed!"

HOLMES: "Human character does evermore publish itself. It will not be concealed." It is impossible to hide the self. Everything we do reveals our character to those around us, whether we talk or remain silent. "When anyone speaks the truth in the spirit of truth, their eye is as clear as the heavens." Liars uncover themselves. We cannot cheat nature or even fool another person for very long. That which we truly are penetrates the masks we wear, and though we take every precaution to conceal insincerity, we will fail. Nature is so organized that we cannot fool it.

"The mind common to all individual people" carries the inner impression of our thought to those with whom we are dealing and subjectively moves their thought to a sure knowledge of our motives. Hence, the unbelief of a lawyer becomes the unbelief of the jury, "despite all their protestations."

We cannot convince others if we are not convinced

ourselves. We cannot give that which we do not possess. We cannot proclaim with conviction what we do not believe. We cannot lie as we would tell the truth, because our own knowledge of our falseness finds a corresponding impression on the hearer. The lie may last for an hour, but truth stands forever, and in the long run "each person passes for that they are worth." "Never a sincere word was utterly lost. Never a magnanimity fell to the ground. Always the heart of humankind greets and accepts it unexpectedly. All people pass for what they are worth. What they are engraves itself on their faces, on their forms, on their fortunes, in letters of light that all may read except themselves. Concealment avails them nothing; boasting, nothing. There is a confession in the glances of their eyes, in their smiles, in salutations and the grasp of hands. Sin bedaubs them, mars all their good impressions. Others know not why they do not trust them, but they do not trust them. Their vice glasses their eyes, demeans their cheeks, pinches the nose, sets the mark of the beast on the back of the head, and writes, O fool! fool! on the forehead of a sovereign."

EMERSON: On the other hand, heroes fear not that if they withhold the avowal of a just and brave act, it will go unwitnessed and unloved. One knows it oneself and is pledged by it to sweetness of peace and to nobleness of aim, which will prove in the end a better proclamation of it than the relating of the incident. Virtue is the adherence in action to the nature of things, and the nature of things makes it prevalent. It consists in a perpetual substitution of being for seeming, and with sublime propriety God is described as saying, *I Am*.

HOLMES: "Virtue is the adherence in action to the nature of things." Virtue is natural. Good is prevalent in nature, and the reason why "God is described as saying, *I Am*" is that God is all-inclusive. The Eternal is absolute, complete, and perfect. It should not be said that God is good as opposed to evil, or timeless as opposed to time, because this suggests opposites to the divine nature. Creator and creation constitute one indivisible wholeness, whose name is *I Am*.

EMERSON: The lesson which these observations convey is, "Be," and not "Seem." Let us acquiesce. Let us take our bloated nothingness out of the path of the divine circuits. Let us unlearn our wisdom of the world. Let us lie low in the Lord's power, and learn that truth alone makes rich and great.

HOLMES: It was a perception of the allness of truth and humankind's complete unity with it that enabled Emerson to say, "The lessons which all these observations convey is, 'Be,' and not 'Seem.'" An external attempt to be thought great is the pretense, while to *be* is to be great. The divine incarnates itself in us. When we live from this God nature, we live in the truth that "makes rich and great."

The petty differences of opinion, the confusion of complicated concepts, the experiences that give the lie to the divine reality are the wisdom of this world. They are false judgments based on a belief in duality. But when we "take our bloated nothingness out of the path of the divine circuits," we are free. This "bloated nothingness" is the false valuation that we place on things. Wealth, conceived as an entity, is a "bloated nothingness." The ambition to promote oneself is "bloated nothingness." Much of our apparent knowledge, our intellectual pon-derosities, may be classed as "bloated nothingness." When the external formality of worship violates the spontaneous expression of instinctive faith, worship be-comes a "bloated nothingness." The pride of fame and name is a "bloated nothingness." Only that which pro-motes the welfare of the soul is profitable. Only that which allows the "divine circuits" to flow unobstructed gives freedom. We are to "lie low in the Lord's power and learn that truth alone makes rich and great."

EMERSON: If you visit your friends, why need you apologize for not having visited them, and waste their time and deface your own act? Visit them now. Let them feel that the highest love has come to see them in thee, its lowest organ. Or why need you torment yourself and them by secret self-reproaches that you have not assisted them or complimented them with gifts and salutations previously? Be a gift and a benediction. Shine with real light, and not with the borrowed reflection of gifts. Common people are apologies for individuals. They bow the head, excuse themselves with prolix reasons, and accumulate appearances because the substance is not.

We are full of these superstitions of sense, the worship of magnitude. We call poets inactive because they are not presidents, merchants, or porters. We adore an institution and do not see that it is founded on a thought which we have. But real action is in silent moments. The epochs of our life are not in the visible facts of our choice of a calling, our marriages, our acquisition of an office, and the like, but in a silent thought by the wayside as we walk, in a thought that revises our entire manner of life and says, "Thus hast thou done, but it were better thus." And all our after years, like menials, serve and wait on this and, according to their ability, execute its will. This revisal or correction is a constant force which, as a tendency, reaches through our lifetime. The object of the person, the aim of these moments, is to make daylight shine through us, to suffer the law to traverse our whole being without obstruction so that, on what point soever of our doing our eye falls, it shall report truly of our character, whether it be our diet, our house, our religious forms, our society, our mirth, our vote, our opposition. Now we are not homogeneous, but heterogeneous, and the ray does not traverse. There are no thorough lights, but the eye of the beholder is puzzled, detecting many unlike tendencies and a life not yet at one.

HOLMES: "Be a gift and a benediction." "Common people are apologies for individuals." God loves not size; whale and minnows are of like dimension. One of Emerson's deepest thoughts was that the Infinite knows no great and no small. Thus, a dignity may be placed upon the slightest act, a compensation found in the smallest pleasure, a true greatness arrived at through the contemplation of a simple truth. The Spirit views everything impersonally and impartially imparts of itself to all.

Those who think great thoughts are great people. They are "dear to the heart of being" because they have allowed the Spirit a free expression through their minds. The possibility of greatness sits at the doorway of everyone's consciousness, silently seeking admission. Thus, the humble is exalted, the valley is lifted to the mountaintop, while "deep cries unto deep."

"Real action is in silent moments." This thought is expressed by many great people preceding Emerson. External acts flow from inner concepts. All our institutions are founded on thought. The "silent thought by the wayside as we walk," which Emerson says "revises our entire manner of life," is the illumination one receives who penetrates objective confusions and subjective differences of opinion. This state of being is apparent throughout all Emerson's writings, an inner awareness of the relationship of the individual mind to the Universal Spirit.

When we have sensed this inner unity in the small moments of our waiting hour, we find that the "aim of these moments is to make daylight shine through us." The light of Spirit will henceforth radiate through our every act. We are twice born. All things take on a new meaning. Life has a greater significance. Our heart now knows that which our intellect could never explain. Nor can the wisdom of humankind confuse, dim, or obliterate this inner light.

Until this moment comes, "we are not homogeneous, but heterogeneous, and the ray does not traverse." While we believe in a spiritual world in one place and a material world in another, in a God external to our souls, in a heaven to be desired and an immortal existence to be obtained, we are not thinking from the standpoint of unity, but of duality. Confusion and blindness follow the "life not yet at one."

EMERSON: Why should we make it a point with our false modesty to disparage that person we are and that form of being assigned to us? A good person is contented. I love and honor Epaminondas, but I do not wish to be Epaminondas. I hold it more just to love the world of this hour than the world of *his* hour. Nor can you, if I am true, excite me to the least uneasiness by saying, "You acted, and thou sittest still." I see action to be good when the need is, and sitting still to be also good. Epaminondas, if he was the person I take him for, would have sat still with joy and peace if his lot had been mine. Heaven is large and affords space for all modes of love and fortitude. Why should we be busybodies and superserviceable? Action and inaction are alike to the true. One piece of the tree is cut for a weathercock, and one for the sleeper of a bridge; the virtue of the wood is apparent in both.

HOLMES: "Action and inaction are alike to the true." Emerson held the moments of contemplation as to be as valuable as those of action. Having theoretically dissolved the material universe, or having resolved it into a spiritual universe, drawing no line between cause and effect, he felt it worthwhile to contemplate his relationship to the Infinite. But unlike many who taught a complete repudiation of the material, Emerson joined life with living, found prayer and performance to be two ends of the same thing, found in nature an answer to the call of the soul, believed action to be good when necessary and inaction to be equally good in those moments when the soul silently weds its self to its source. "Heaven is large and affords space for all modes of love and fortitude."

EMERSON: I desire not to disgrace the soul. The fact that I am here certainly shows me that the soul had need of an organ here. Shall I not assume the post? Shall I skulk and dodge and duck with my unseasonable apologies and vain modesty, and imagine my being here impertinent, less pertinent than Epaminondas or Homer being there, and that the soul did not know its own needs? Besides, without any reasoning on the matter, I have no discontent. The good soul nourishes me and unlocks new magazines of power and enjoyment to me every day. I will not meanly decline the immensity of good, because I have heard that it has come to others in another shape.

HOLMES: "The fact that I am here certainly shows me that the soul had need of an organ here." The objective world is a necessary expression of the Spirit. We would not have bodies if we did not need them, and we should not question the integrity of the soul that has projected the body.

We must learn to accept ourselves for better or for worse, to trust the divine nature inherent in our own being, and to live from this divine nature alone.

EMERSON: Besides, why should we be cowed by the name of Action? 'Tis a trick of the senses; no more. We know that the ancestor of every action is a thought. The poor mind does not seem to itself to be anything, unless it have an outside badge, some Gentoo diet or Quaker coat or Calvinistic prayer-meeting or philanthropic society or a great donation or a high office or, anyhow, some wild contrasting action to testify that it is somewhat. The rich mind lies in the sun and sleeps, and is Nature. To think is to act.

HOLMES: "The ancestor of every action is a thought." The external badge, the prayer meeting, or philosophic society is evidence of this fact. The Creator is within. Hence, "the rich mind lies in the sun and sleeps, and is nature."

EMERSON: Let us, if we must have great actions, make our own so. All action is of an infinite elasticity, and the least admits of being inflated with the celestial air until it eclipses the sun and moon. Let us seek one peace by fidelity. Let me heed my duties. Why need I go gadding into the scenes and philosophy of Greek and Italian history, before I have justified myself to my benefactors? How dare I read Washington's campaigns, when I have not answered the letters of my own correspondents? Is not that a just objection to much of our reading? It is a pusillanimous desertion of our work to gaze after our neighbors. It is peeping. Byron says of Jack Bunting, "He knew not what to say, and so he swore."

I may say it of our preposterous use of books, "They knew not what to do, and so they read." I can think of nothing to fill my time with, and I find the Life of Brant. It is a very extravagant compliment to pay to Brant, or to General Schuyler or to General Washington. My time should be as good as their time; my facts, my net of relations as good as theirs, or either of theirs. Rather let me do my work so well that other idlers, if they choose, may compare my texture with the texture of these and find it identical with the best.

HOLMES: "Let us, if we must have great actions, make our own so." Only that is great to us which we make great. The greatness of others is ours when we ourselves are great. "All action is of infinite elasticity." A potential possibility is inherent in everything that the Infinite projects, and since we are incarnations of the Infinite, we are equipped with limitless possibilities. When our minds are "inflated with the celestial air," that is, when we are in accord with the divine will and purpose, we are powerful and complete.

Since each individual is an inlet to this "celestial air," we need not "go gaddying into the scenes of philosophy" of others, because we have within ourselves the same scenes and philosophies. We unduly honor those whom we call great and extend to them "a very extravagant complement" when we feel that our entire time must be spent in studying their lives, thoughts, and actions, rather than in the contemplation of our own being, in the careful searching of our own souls, for the Infinite

Originator. When we do this, we find that the tincture
of our own soul is "identical with the best."

EMERSON: This overestimate of the possibilities
of Paul and Pericles, this underestimate of our own,
comes from a neglect of the fact of an identical nature.
Bonaparte knew but one merit, and rewarded in one and
the same way the good soldier, the good astronomer, the
good poet, the good player. The poet uses the names
of Caesar, of Tamerlane, of Bonduca, of Belisarius. The
painter uses the conventional story of the Virgin Mary,
of Paul, of Peter. They do not, therefore, defer to the
nature of these accidental people, of these stock heroes.
If poets write a true drama, then they are Caesar and
not the player of Caesar. Then, the selfsame strain of
thought, emotion as pure, wit as subtle, motions as swift,
mounting, extravagant, and a heart as great, self-suffic-
ing, dauntless, which on the waves of its love and hope
can uplift all that is reckoned solid and precious in the
world—palaces, gardens, money, navies, realms—mark-
ing its own incomparable worth by the slight it casts on
these gauds of people—these all are theirs, and by the
power of these, they rouse the nations. Let a person believe in God, and not in names and places and people.
Let the great soul incarnated in some person's form, poor
and sad and single, go out to service and sweep chambers
and scour floors, and its effulgent daybeams cannot be

muffled or hid, but to sweep and scour will instantly appear supreme and beautiful actions, the top and radiance of human life, and all people will get mops and brooms until, lo! suddenly the great soul has enshrined itself in some other form and done some other deed, and that is now the flower and head of all living nature.

HOLMES: "This overestimate of the possibilities of Paul and Pericles, this underestimate of our own, comes from a neglect of the fact of an identical nature." It is this "identical nature" which Emerson emphasizes in all his writings—this "mind common to all individuals." Because of this "identical nature," the spiritual background of every person is the same. The source of all life is one, though its manifestations may be varied. These varied manifestations are merely the play of life upon itself. Hence, "if poets write a true drama, then they are Caesar," because, looking back into the depth of being itself, the poet, Caesar, or nature are all God. It is through the power of this God-being inherent in us that we live, imagine, and create. "These are all ours, and by the power of these, we rouse the nations."

Again, Emerson says, "But the great names cannot stead us if we have not life itself." The great names are, to us, what we bring to them. Life is what we make it, height and depth, hope and despair, heaven and hell. When we believe "in God, and not in names and places and persons," "suddenly the great soul has enshrined itself in some other form," pure, original. "The great soul," which is the divine nature, comes to us in the silence of our own thought, comes in the performance of our act, in the contemplation of our being, and in the outward swing of completion. Flowing into the receptive mind, it floods the intellect, surges through the emotion, and finds an extension of itself in us, as the Universal passes into action through the human.

EMERSON: We are the photometers, we the irritable goldleaf and tinfoil that measure the accumulations of the subtle element. We know the authentic effects of the true fire through every one of its million disguises.

HOLMES: Through all the multiplied forms of life runs one thread of unity. "The subtle element," the divine stuff of every form. The one passes into the all. The all is resolvable again to the one, while those spiritual laws that execute themselves, servants of the mind that lies stretched "in smiling repose," are always operative.

We are surrounded by an infinite reality, a limitless possibility, a creative genius so stupendous that our imagination is staggered as we contemplate it. This Infinite is One, the Original Flame, and "we know the authentic effects of the true fire through every one of its million disguises."

HISTORY

History

The Universal Spirit knows neither great nor small. It is not comparative. It creates all and is present in all. All things are dear to the heart of its being. It is as manifest in the wayside flower as in a system of planets. The infinite is not big in one place and little in another, but is equally distributed, omnipresent, always available. It is both cause and effect, both creator and that which is created.

RALPH WALDO EMERSON: There is one mind common to all individuals. Everyone is an inlet to the same and to all of the same. They that are once admitted to the right of reason are made masters of the whole estate. What Plato has thought, all may think; what a saint has felt, all may feel; what at any time has befallen anyone, all can understand. Who hath access to this universal mind is a party to all that is or can be done, for this is the only and sovereign agent.

ERNEST HOLMES: Emerson starts his essay on "History" with this bold declaration: "There is one mind common to all individuals." The mind of God and the mind of the individual are one and the same.

Somewhere in the cryptic depths of human nature, the Divine Mind reveals itself. This mind is the one real agent behind all human endeavors, stimulating all individual thought.

EMERSON: Of the works of this mind, history is the record. Its genius is illustrated by the entire series of days. Humankind is explicable by nothing less than all its history. Without hurry, without rest, the human spirit goes forth from the beginning to embody every faculty, every thought, every emotion which belongs to it in appropriate events. But the thought is always prior to the fact; all the facts of history preexist in the mind as laws. Each law in turn is made by circumstances predominant, and the limits of nature give power to but one at a time. An individual is the whole encyclopedia of facts. The creation of a thousand forests is in one acorn, and Egypt, Greece, Rome, Gaul, Britain, and America lie folded already in the first human. Epoch after epoch, camp, realm, empire, republic, democracy are merely the application of our manifold spirit to the manifold world.

HOLMES: "Of the works of this mind, history is the record." History is the impress that the Universal Mind makes on the individual life. History is an objective manifestation of subtle subjective and spiritual causes. The cause is hidden; the effect is obvious.

"All the facts of history preexist in the mind as laws." The creative impulse is spiritual, while its manifestation is always in accord with law. Behind the facts of history is the impulse of the Spirit emerging through law and order. Since everyone's mind is rooted in the infinite, the Universal Mind is to be interpreted to all, through all, and in no other way.

EMERSON: This human mind wrote history, and this must read it. The Sphinx must solve its own riddle. If the whole of history is in one person, it is all to be explained from individual experience. There is a relation between the hours of our lives and the centuries of time. As the air I breathe is drawn from the great repositories of nature, as the light on my book is yielded by a star a hundred millions of miles distant, as the poise of my body depends on the equilibrium of centrifugal and centripetal forces, so the hours should be instructed by the ages and the ages explained by the hours. Of the universal mind, each individual is one more incarnation. All its properties consist in the individual. Each new fact in the individual's private experience flashes a light on what great bodies of people have done, and the crises of the individual's life refer to national crises. Every revolution was first a thought in one person's mind, and when the same thought occurs to another, it is the key to that era. Every reform was once a private opinion, and when it shall be a private opinion again, it will solve the problem of the age. The fact narrated must correspond to something in me to be credible or intelligible. We, as we read, must become Greeks, Romans, Turks, priest and sovereign, martyr and executioner, must fasten these images to some reality in our secret experience, or we shall learn nothing rightly. What befell Asdrubal or Caesar Borgia is as much an illustration of the mind's powers and depravations as what has befallen us. Each new law and political movement has meaning for you. Stand before each of its tablets and say, "Under this mask did my Proteus nature hide itself." This remedies the defect of our too great nearness to ourselves. This throws our actions into perspective, and as crabs, goats, scorpions, the balance and the water pot lose their meanness when hung as signs in the zodiac, so I can see my own vices without heat in the distant persons of Solomon, Alcibiades and Catiline.

HOLMES: "This human mind wrote history, and this must read it. The sphinx must solve its own riddle." The mind that stimulated the acts of antiquity is the same mind that is stimulating our present acts. It emerges through all. It embraces all ages, encompasses all periods, is present at all times. Uncreated, it creates; unformed, it gives form; unborn, it gives birth. Each hour of our day is an hour of its day. The universal law that holds everything in place is the government of this mind.

"Of the universal mind, each individual is one more incarnation. All of its properties consist in the individual." That is, every person contains the divine properties. All are patterned after the original creative genius. All are divine by nature, not by choice. It is through the unity of all minds with the one Mind that we are to interpret history. This interpretation is possible because there is within us the same motive that has stimulated other people's thought. We understand their motives through an understanding of our own mental reactions to life.

We read the story of our own impulses in Solomon and Cataline. All human laws find their origin and ultimate reason for being in the Universal Mind. Hence, the laws of justice and righteousness do not change, though we may reinterpret them, each in our own tongue. We understand what others have done because there is something in us akin to others, no matter in what age they may have lived. The power that stimulates the poet, the artist, and the artisan is ours. We are born at home with all people by reason of the mind common to all people.

I in they, and they in me, that I may become one in Thee. Then the Word becomes flesh and dwells among us.

EMERSON: It is the universal nature which gives worth to particular people and things. Human life as containing this is mysterious and inviolable, and we hedge it round with penalties and laws. All laws derive hence their ultimate reason; all express more or less distinctly some command of this supreme, illimitable essence. Property also holds of the soul, covers great spiritual facts, and instinctively we at first hold to it with swords and laws, and wide and complex combinations. The obscure consciousness of this fact is the light of all our day, the claim of claims: the plea for education, for justice, for charity, the foundation of friendship and love, and of the heroism and grandeur which belong to acts of self-reliance. It is remarkable that, involuntarily, we always read as superior beings. Universal history, the poets, the romancers do not in their stateliest pictures—in the sacerdotal, the imperial palaces, in the triumphs of will or of genius—anywhere lose our ear, anywhere make us feel that we intrude, that this is for better people. But rather is it true that in their grandest strokes we feel most at home. All that Shakespeare says of the sovereign, yonder slip of a child that reads in the corner feels to be true of himself. We sympathize in the great moments of history, in the great discoveries, the great resistances, the great prosperities of others, because there law was enacted, the sea was searched, the land was found or the blow was struck for us, as we ourselves in that place would have done or applauded.

We have the same interest in condition and character. We honor the rich because they have externally the freedom, power, and grace that we feel to be proper to all people, proper to us. So all that is said of the wise by Stoic or Oriental or modern essayist describes to all readers their own ideas, describes their unattained but attainable selves. All literature writes the character of the wise. Books, monuments, pictures, conversation are portraits in which the wise find the lineaments they are forming. The silent and the eloquent praise them and accost them, and they are stimulated wherever they move as by personal allusions. True aspirants, therefore, never need look for allusions personal and laudatory in discourse. They hear the commendation not of themselves, but more sweet, of that character they see in every word that is said concerning character, yea, further, in every fact and circumstance—in the running river and the rustling corn. Praise is looked, homage tendered, love flows from mute nature, from the mountains and the lights of the firmament.

HOLMES: "All that Shakespeare says of the sovereign, yonder slip of a child that reads in the corner, feels to be true of himself." Of the infinite variety of characterizations possible to the Universal Mind, Shakespeare was a masterful interpreter, able to place himself in thousand different lights before the one animating intelligence, that it might personify itself through the innumerable forms for him. The child, as it reads, instinctively senses itself in these characterizations. The child enters into the play because the play has already entered into the child. That which another wrote now emerges through the child.

Mind knows no great and no small, no yesterday and no tomorrow, and since it is forever present and is the mind common to all people, "all the facts of history pre-exist in the mind as laws." Therefore, Emerson tells us, "The blow was struck for us." The rich person reveals the opulence of our own being. The philosopher plumbs a deep in our own soul. Nature gives us back to ourselves. Emerson felt the unity of all, the oneness of the Universal Spirit with the individual soul. He sensed the invisible tie that binds all to all.

EMERSON: These hints, dropped as it were from sleep and night, let us use in broad day. Students are to read history actively and not passively, to esteem their own life the text, and books the commentary. Thus compelled, the muse of history will utter oracles, as never to those who do not respect themselves. I have no expectation that anyone will read history aright who thinks that what was done in a remote age by those whose names have resounded far has any deeper sense than what we are doing today.

HOLMES: We are to read history actively, not passively, not to think of history as a story of past events only, but as an activity experienced in our present life— a picture drawn for us, a movement created for our amusement. The stage setting is the world. We create the playing, assume the leading role, and, at same time, are our own audience.

The crowning of a castle or the laying of a cornerstone for a cottage are of equal importance to the Cosmic Mind. We perceive the significance of others only through a true appreciation of our own. The most trivial act that constructively expresses the individual life has as deep a significance as the creation of an empire. Emerson gives any supreme importance to the individual life.

We each must be conscious of our own worth. We must know that what we have placed in the universal scheme of things is essential to its expression. Without the individual, God would be incomplete.

EMERSON: The world exists for the education of the individual. There is no age or state of society or mode of action in history to which there is not somewhat correspondence in our own life. Everything tends in a wonderful manner to abbreviate itself and yield its own virtue to us. We should see that we can live all history in our own person. We must sit solidly at home and not suffer ourselves to be bullied by sovereigns or empires, but know that we are greater than all the geography and all the government of the world. We must transfer the point of view from which history is commonly read, from Rome and Athens and London to ourselves, and not deny our conviction that we are the court. If England or Egypt have anything to say to us, we will try the case. If not, let them forever be silent. We must attain and maintain that lofty sight where facts yield their secret sense, and poetry and annals are alike. The instinct of the mind—the purpose of nature—betrays itself in the use we make of the signal narrations of history. Time dissipates to shining ether the solid angularity of facts. No anchor, no cable, no fences avail to keep a fact a fact. Babylon, Troy, Tyre, Palestine, and even early Rome are passing already into fiction. The Garden of Eden, the sun standing still in Gibeon, is poetry thenceforward to all nations. Who cares what the fact was, when we have made a constellation of it to hang in heaven an immortal sign? London and Paris and New York must go the same way. "What is history," said Napoleon, "but a fable agreed upon?" This life of ours is stuck round with Egypt, Greece, Gaul, England, war, colonization, church, court, and commerce, as with so many flowers and wild ornaments grave and gay. I will not make more account of them. I believe in eternity. I can find Greece, Asia, Italy, Spain, and the Islands, the genius and creative principle of each and of all eras, in my own mind.

HOLMES: "The world exists for the education of all people." Psychology teaches that our subjective reactions encompass the entire history of the human race, that our contact with the race mind is a tremendous influence in our lives. Emerson sensed the "something" about humankind that encompasses all ages. Thus, to each person does it "abbreviate itself and yield its own virtue to them." We must know that we are greater than the vast panorama of human existence and experience, whether we think of experience as extended into the past, unfolding through the present, or penetrating into the future.

The human drama is interior, never external. Our appreciation of these interior facts constitutes the only validity they can have for us. We transcend them all. From this viewpoint alone can these facts "yield their secret sense." The facts themselves are fluid.

History is already a stream merged with the ocean of life. It is rain mingled with the wave. The essential worth of any fact finds true significance in a combination of all facts, thus creating new tendencies toward greater accomplishments. As history is "but a fable agreed upon," so present facts will soon melt into the general landscape of human experiences, each significant, but none too important.

The perspective of eternity alone satisfies. Eternity encompasses all facts, is the melting pot of all experiences, the creator of all. It is the principal animating all. Creator and creation are one. God and humankind are one. Hence, Emerson says, "the genius and creative principle of each and all eras, I can find in my own mind." We will misunderstand Emerson entirely unless we realize that he felt himself to be a projection of the Original Mind. To him, the human is more than an impersonation of the divine; it *is* the divine.

EMERSON: We are always coming up with the emphatic facts of history in our private experience and verifying them here. All history becomes subjective. In other words, there is properly no history, only biography. Every mind must know the whole lesson for itself, must go over the whole ground. What it does not see, what it does not live, it will not know. What the former age has epitomized into a formula or rule for manipular convenience, it will lose all the good of verifying for itself by means of the wall of that rule. Somewhere, sometime, it will demand and find compensation for that loss by doing the work itself. Ferguson discovered many things in astronomy which had long been known. The better for him.

History must be this, or it is nothing. Every law which the state enacts indicates a fact in human nature; that is all. We must in ourselves see the necessary reason of every fact, see how it could and must be. So stand before every public and private work, before an oration of Burke, before a victory of Napoleon, before a martyrdom of Sir Thomas More, of Sidney, of Marmaduke Robinson, before a French Reign of Terror and a Salem hanging of witches, before a fanatic Revival and the Animal Magnetism in Paris, or in Providence. We assume that we, under like influence, should be alike affected and should achieve the like, and we aim to master intellectually the steps and reach the same height or the same degradation that our neighbor, our proxy, has done.

HOLMES: "All history becomes subjective. In other words, there is properly no history; only biography." History is more than an external fact. It marks the evolution of personality. What we cannot see, know, and experience, we cannot understand. We feel historic events emerging through our own impulses, the result of our own passion. It is the history of our own lives. The facts only are external. They are already subjective in our being.

When the facts of history fit nicely into some niche in our own mind, we understand their meaning. If we could remove the mask from the face of Sir Thomas Moore, The Reign of Terror, or the fanatic Revival, we would see things standing as proxies to ourselves. The soul encompasses all experiences, impersonates all characters, institutes all religions, and creates all governments. We stand on the mountain top and descend into hell by the natural affinity of our own souls. We are both saint and sinner, the savior and the condemned.

Again, let us remember that Emerson is speaking of the Universal Mind incarnated alike in each. Being a subjective unit, it remains true to its own nature, even though incarnated in innumerable personalities. The thread of its being runs in an unbroken stream of consciousness through our mentalities, each in all and all in each.

EMERSON: All inquiry into antiquity—all curiosity respecting the Pyramids, the excavated cities, Stonehenge, the Ohio Circles, Mexico, Memphis—is the desire to do away this wild, savage, and preposterous There or Then, and introduce in its place the Here and the

Now. Belzoni digs and measures in the mummy-pits and pyramids of Thebes until he can see the end of the difference between the monstrous work and himself. When he has satisfied himself, in general and in detail, that it was made by such a person as he, so armed and so motivated, and to ends to which he himself should also have worked, the problem is solved. His thought lives along the whole line of temples and sphinxes and catacombs, passes through them all with satisfaction, and they live again to the mind, or are now.

A Gothic cathedral affirms that it was done by us and not done by us. Surely it was by an individual, but we find it not in our individuality. But we apply ourselves to the history of its production. We put ourselves into the place and state of the builder. We remember the forest-dwellers, the first temples, the adherence to the first type, and the decoration of it as the wealth of the nation increased. The value which is given to wood by carving led to the carving over the whole mountain of stone of a cathedral. When we have gone through this process and added thereto the Catholic Church, its cross, its music, its processions, its Saints' days, and image-worship, we have, as it were, been the one who made the minister. We have seen how it could and must be. We have the sufficient reason.

HOLMES: "We have, as it were, been the one who made the minister." Our inquiries into antiquity are for the purpose of transposing the "there and then" into the "here and now." The "there and then" and the "here and now" are alike. All events are the same to the mind that stretches into the past, comprehends the present, and measures the possibilities of the future. The mind stands still while all movement takes place within it. Antiquity reveals what we might have done. Current events portray our present states of thought. The possibility of the future is already inherent in our imagination.

We are satisfied when we uncover the ego. We find that all people have acted as we act. "The problem is then solved." As our thought merges through appreciation of others into their environment and into the emotions stimulating their acts, we understand the meaning of those acts. Moreover, we realize that each act was necessary for the occasion, adequate for the time, and justified by the necessity of the case.

Religion, poetry, art, philosophy, science, invention, the minister and the congregation, Jesus, the Catholic Church and image-worship all reveal the eloquent soul expressing itself through multiform practices. Looking deep into our own natures, "we have the sufficient reason."

EMERSON: The difference between individuals is in their principle of association. Some people classify objects by color and size and other accidents of appearance; others, by intrinsic likeness or by the relation of cause and effect. The progress of the intellect is to the clearer vision of causes, which neglects surface differences. To the poet, to the philosopher, to the saint, all things are friendly and sacred, all events profitable, all days holy, all people divine, because the eye is fastened on the life and slights the circumstance. Every chemical substance, every plant, every animal in its growth teaches the unity of cause, the variety of appearance.

HOLMES: "The progress of the intellect consists in the clearer vision of causes, which overlooks surface differences." While the intellect remains on the surface of life, viewing disassociated facts and measuring differences of opinion, it fails to penetrate the unitary cause, the thread of beauty running through all. To the one whose vision penetrates through externals, all things become holy and "all people divine."

All have one the common origin in the "one mind common to the individual." Unity passes into multiplicity, and the one may be expressed through the many. Everyone's life is divine at the root. The philosophic problem of "the one and the many" is solved when we understand that the many emerges from the one. Infinite potentiality produces limitless variations of itself. The cause is generic and the expression individual, but since all effect is rooted in one cause, unity runs through variety, binding all together in one common wholeness.

EMERSON: Upborn and surrounded as we are by this all-creating nature, soft and fluid as a cloud or the air, why should we be such hard pedants and magnify a few forms? Why should we make account of time or of magnitude or of figure? The soul knows them not, and genius, obeying its law, knows how to play with them as a young child plays with graybeards and in churches. Genius studies the causal thought and, far back in the womb of things, sees the rays parting from one orb, that diverge ere they fall by infinite diameters. Genius watches the monad through all its masks as it performs the metempsychosis of nature. Genius detects through the fly, through the caterpillar, through the grub, through the egg, the constant individual; through countless individuals, the fixed species; through many species, the genus; through all genera, the steadfast type; through all the realms of organized life, the eternal unity. Nature is a mutable cloud, which is always and never the same. It casts the same thought into troops of forms as a poet makes twenty fables with one moral. Through the bruteness and toughness of matter, a subtle spirit bends all things to its own will. The adamant streams into soft but precise form before it, and whilst I look at it, its outline and texture are changed again. Nothing is so fleeting as form, yet never does it quite deny itself. In humankind, we still trace the remains or hints of all that we esteem badges of servitude in the lower races; yet in us, they enhance our nobleness and grace, as Io in *Aeschylus,* transformed to a cow, offends the imagination. But how changed, when as Isis in Egypt, she meets Osiris-Jove, a beautiful woman, with nothing of the metamorphosis left but the lunar horns as the splendid ornament of her brows!

HOLMES: "Genius studies the casual thought." Emerson sees through the hard facts into the "soft and fluid." Nature is a hard fact. Its cause is a fluidic presence solidifying into definite form for the purpose of self-expression. The fact is transitory; the fluid eternal. Time is only a measure of eternity, melting at each end into the backward flow of the past and into the onward flow of the future. The present is only a point in this eternal flow.

In the attempt to place our finger on the hard fact of the present, we find the flow of an invisible cause already moving the present into the past and introducing the future. The finger points to one place; the flow knows no place, no time, only being. Humankind places the time, as with events, as "far back in the womb of things, sees the rays parting from one orb."

Nature wears a mask that, if it could be lifted, would reveal the central principle, forever the same "through countless individuals." Through all the variations of nature runs "the eternal unity," the everlasting will and purpose of the universe, the omnipresent good. Half concealed, nature reveals itself through an inner sense that all have but few use.

The mask is lifted. The many melt into the one, the one emerges through the many, and the vast panorama of human existence—all types, all species of the realms of organized life—fuse together in one stupendous whole. Identity and form remain, yet constantly change and evolve. A thing is never twice alike. Creation is a constant progress impelled by a continuous urge, propelled by a dynamic power, and held in place through an infinite will and purpose and an immutable law.

EMERSON: The identity of history is equally intrinsic, the diversity equally obvious. There is at the surface infinite variety of things; at the center there is simplicity of cause. How many are the acts of one individual in which we recognize the same character! Observe the sources of our information in respect to the Greek genius. We have the civil history of that people, as Herodotus, Thucydides, Xenophon, and Plutarch have given it, a very sufficient account of what manner of persons they were and what they did. We have the same national mind expressed for us again in their literature, in epic and lyric poems, drama and philosophy, a very complete form. Then we have it once more in their architecture, a beauty as of temperance itself, limited to the straight line and the square, a builded geometry. Then we have it once again in sculpture, the "tongue on the balance of expression," a multitude of forms in the utmost freedom of action, and never transgressing the ideal serenity, but like votaries performing some religious dance before the gods, and though in convulsive pain or mortal combat, never daring to break the figure and decorum of their dance. Thus, of the genius of one remarkable people, we have a four-fold representation, and to the senses what more unlike than an ode of Pindar, a marble centaur, the peristyle of the Parthenon, and the last actions of Phocion?

Everyone must have observed faces and forms which, without any resembling feature, make a like impression on the beholder. A particular picture or copy of verses, if it does not awaken the same train of images, will yet super-induce the same sentiment as some wild mountain walk, although the resemblance is nowise obvious to the senses, but is occult and out of the reach of the under-standing. Nature is an endless combination and repetition of a very few laws. It hums the old well-known air through innumerable variations.

HOLMES: "There is at the surface infinite variety of things; at the center, there is simplicity and unity of cause." Just as we can imagine innumerable situations and still maintain the integrity of our individuality, so the unitary cause never departs from the simplicity of oneness, even though it passes into a variety of forms.

The psychology of humanity is revealed in its art, literature, and government. The psychology of one age bears a likeness to that of another. "Nature...hums the old well-known air through innumerable variations."

EMERSON: Nature is full of a sublime family likeness throughout its works and delights in startling us with resemblances in the most unexpected quarters. I have seen the head of an old sachem of the forest, which at once reminded the eye of a bald mountain summit, and the furrows of the brow suggested the strata of the rock. There are people whose manners have the same essential splendor as the simple and awful sculpture on the friezes of the Parthenon and the remains of the earliest Greek art. And there are compositions of the same strain to be found in the books of all ages. What is Guido's Rospigliosi Aurora but a morning thought, as the horses in it are only a morning cloud. If anyone will but take pains to observe the variety of actions to which they are equally inclined in certain moods of mind and those to which they are averse, they will see how deep is the chain of affinity.

A painter told me that nobody could draw a tree without in some sort becoming a tree, or draw a child by studying the outlines of its form merely. But by watching for a time their motions and plays, painters enter into their natures and can then draw them at will in every attitude. So Roos "entered into the inmost nature of a sheep." I knew a drafter employed in a public survey who found that he could not sketch the rocks until their geological structure was first explained to him. In a certain state of thought is the common origin of very diverse works. It is the spirit and not the fact that is identical. By a deeper apprehension and not primarily by a painful acquisition of many manual skills, the artist attains the power of awakening other souls to a given activity.

HOLMES: "It is the Spirit and not the fact that is identical." If all facts were identical, nature would become a monotony without variation, the unity would be bored by its own sameness, and life would be unbearable. It is the Spirit that is identical; the fact is a passing fancy. Our emotions may change, and the shifting scenes of time flow on into newer and greater experiences, into diversified results and accomplishments. But always the soft presence of the interior Spirit reveals its identity.

We never appear to be the same in any two instances. We are never other than the same. The eternal thing within us, which is God, is the "chain of affinity" revealing us to ourselves. A universal theme runs through all literature. A naturalist melts into the tree, the lover of animals finds a communion of soul with them, the geologist reads in the rocks a self-identity, and the artist awakens to self-revelation through art.

EMERSON: It has been said, that "common souls pay with what they do; nobler souls with that which they are." And why? Because a profound nature awakens in us by its actions and words, by its very looks and manners, the same power and beauty that a gallery of sculpture or of pictures addresses.

Civil and natural history, the history of art and of literature, must be explained from individual history, or must remain words. There is nothing but is related to us, nothing that does not interest us. Realm, college, tree, horse, or iron shoe, the roots of all things are in humankind. Santa Croce and the Dome of St. Peter's are lame copies after a divine model. Strasburg Cathedral is a material counterpart of the soul of Erwin of Steinbach. The true poem is the poet's mind; the true ship is the ship-builder. In individuals, could we lay them open, we should see the reason for the last flourish and tendril of their work, as every spine and tint in the seashell preexist in the secreting organs of the fish. The whole of heraldry and of chivalry is in courtesy. A person of fine manners shall pronounce your name with all the ornament that titles of nobility could ever add.

HOLMES: "Common souls pay with what they do; nobler souls with that which they all are." Being is greater than becoming. We sense in great and noble souls an interior source and inner calm that comes to them through constant communion with the Universal Spirit.

The presence of beauty bespeaks its own loveliness. It is not alone through external acts that the individual is revealed. The individual is truly revealed when the actor melts into the act, when action becomes an eloquent gesture of the immovable soul.

EMERSON: The trivial experience of every day is always verifying some old prediction to us and converting into things the words and signs which we had heard and seen without heed. A friend with whom I was riding in the forest said to me that the woods always seemed to her to wait, as if the genies who inhabit them suspended their deeds until the wayfarer has passed onward, a thought which poetry has celebrated in the dance of the fairies that breaks off on the approach of human feet. The individual who has seen the rising moon break out of the clouds at midnight has been present like an archangel at the creation of light and of the world. I remember one summer day in the fields, my companion pointed out to me a broad cloud, which might extend a quarter of a mile parallel to the horizon, quite accurately in the form of a cherub as painted over churches, a round block in the center that it was easy to animate with eyes and mouth, supported on either side by wide-stretched symmetrical wings. What appears once in the atmosphere may appear often, and it was undoubtedly the archetype of that familiar ornament. I have seen in the sky a chain of summer lightning which at once showed to me that the Greeks drew from nature when they painted the thunderbolt in the hand of Jove. I have seen a snow-drift along the sides of the stone wall which obviously gave the idea of the common architectural scroll to abut a tower.

HOLMES: "In individuals, could we lay them open, we should see the sufficient reason." Emerson based his philosophy on theory that life flows from within. Hence, he says, "It is in the soul that architecture exists." The true poem is a poet's mind. The subjective state of our thought decides the tendency of our objective experience, sets a gauge to the possibility of our achievement, and controls our destiny.

The soul is the medium between the absolute and relative. Everything begins with an idea. Emerson draws no line between the word of God and the word of the individual. He believes the difference is not in essence, but in degree. Could we see inside people, we should find subjective imagery exactly balancing their objective accomplishments.

EMERSON: By surrounding ourselves with the original circumstances, we invent anew the orders and the ornaments of architecture, as we see how each person merely decorated their primitive abodes. The Doric temple preserves the semblance of the wooden cabin in which the Dorian dwelt. The Chinese pagoda is plainly a Tartar tent. The Indian and Egyptian temples still betray the mounds and subterranean houses of their ancestors. "The custom of making houses and tombs in the living rock," says Heeren in his *Researches on the Ethiopians*, "determined very naturally the principal character of the Nubian Egyptian architecture to the colossal form which it assumed. In these caverns, already prepared by nature, the eye was accustomed to dwell on huge shapes and masses, so that when art came to the assistance of nature, it could not move on a small scale without degrading itself. What would statues of the usual size, or neat porches and wings, have been, associated with those gigantic halls before which only Colossi could sit as watchers, or lean on the pillars of the interior?"

The Gothic church plainly originated in a rude adaptation of the forest trees with all their boughs to a festal or solemn arcade, as the bands about the cleft pillars still indicate the green withes that tied them. No one can walk in a road cut through pine woods without being struck with the architectural appearance of the grove, especially in winter when the bareness of all other trees shows the low arch of the Saxons. In the woods in a winter afternoon, one will see as readily the origin of the stained-glass window, with which the Gothic cathedrals are adorned, in the colors of the western sky seen through the bare and crossing branches of the forest. Nor can any lover of nature enter the old piles of Oxford and the English cathedrals without feeling that the forest overpowered the mind of the builder, and that the builder's chisel, saw, and plane still reproduced its ferns, its spikes of flowers, its locust, elm, oak, pine, fir, and spruce.

HOLMES: These paragraphs show the original architect dwelling in nature. Our patterns are instinctively drawn from its mind, but since the two minds are one, we need not leave the precincts of our own thought in drawing from the deep reservoir. The creator is forever passing into creation; being is forever in a process of becoming.

EMERSON: The Gothic cathedral is a blossoming in stone subdued by the insatiable demand of harmony in humankind. The mountain of granite blooms into an eternal flower, with the lightness and delicate finish, as well as the aerial proportions and perspective, of vegetable beauty.

HOLMES: The trees have souls; the intelligence that creates the forest and the flowers, builds the temple— "a blossoming in stone." Nature individualizes itself. The divine passes into the most commonplace object. "The mountain of granite blooms into an eternal flower." The whole theme is unity and variety— variety within unity.

EMERSON: In like manner, all public facts are to be individualized; all private facts are to be generalized. Then at once history becomes fluid and true, and biography deep and sublime. As the Persians imitated in the slender shafts and capitals of their architecture the stem and flower of the lotus and palm, so the Persian court in its magnificent era never gave over the nomadism of its barbarous tribes, but travelled from Ecbatana where the spring was spent, to Susa in summer and to Babylon for the winter.

HOLMES: "All public facts are to be individualized; all private facts are to be generalized." The human race is composed of individuals. The human race, acting as a whole, is a generalization of individual minds. The individual, acting as a unit, is an individualization of the race mind. All are rooted in the fundamental unit. To interpret the stream of consciousness running through human events is to understand history. Individual biography—the motives and incentives of personal action—is understood when we link the individual stream of consciousness with the collective and to the universal streams.

EMERSON: In the early history of Asia and Africa, nomadism and agriculture are the two antagonist facts. The geography of Asia and of Africa necessitated a nomadic life, but the nomads were the terror of all those whom the soil, or the advantages of a market, had induced to build towns. Agriculture, therefore, was a religious injunction because of the perils of the state from nomadism. In these late and civil countries of England and America, these propensities still fight out the old battle in the nation and in the individual. The nomads of Africa were constrained to wander by the attacks of the gadfly, which drives the cattle mad and so compels the tribe to emigrate in the rainy season and to drive off the cattle to the higher sandy regions. The nomads of Asia follow the pasturage from month to month. In America and Europe, the nomadism is of trade and curiosity, a progress certainly from the gadfly of Astaboras to the Anglo and Italo-mania of Boston Bay. Sacred cities, to which a periodical religious pilgrimage was enjoined, or stringent laws and customs tending to invigorate the national bond, were the check on the old rovers, and the cumulative values of long residence are the restraints on the itinerancy of the present day. The antagonism of the two tendencies is not less active in individuals, as the love of adventure or the love of repose happens to predominate. Those of rude health and flowing spirits have the faculty of rapid domestication, live in their wagons and roam through all latitudes as easily as a Calmuc. At sea or in the forest or in the snow, they sleep as warm, dine with as good appetite, and associate as happily as beside their own chimneys. Or perhaps their facility is deeper seated in the increased range of their faculties of observation, which yield them points of interest wherever fresh objects meet their eyes. The pastoral nations were needy and hungry to desperation, and this intellectual nomadism, in its excess, bankrupts the mind through the dissipation of power on a miscellany of objects. The home-keeping wit, on the other hand, is that continence or content which finds all the elements of life in its own soil and which has its own perils of monotony and deterioration if not stimulated by foreign infusions.

HOLMES: The instant demand of nature arouses our curiosity, stimulates us to accomplishment, and pushes us from one position into another with an irresistible demand. Unity must pass into variety. All nature is unified at the center. Those who are in rapport with it find a table spread before them in the wilderness, are at home on the sea, have fellowship with the forest, and "everywhere fall into easy relations with their neighbor."

EMERSON: Everything individuals see without them corresponds to their states of mind, and everything is in turn intelligible to them as their onward thinking leads them into the truth to which that fact or series belongs.

The primeval world—the "fore-world," as the Germans say—I can dive to it in myself as well as grope for it with researching fingers in catacombs, libraries, and the broken reliefs and torsos of ruined villas.

What is the foundation of that interest all people feel in Greek history, letters, art, and poetry, in all its periods from the Heroic or Homeric age down to the domestic life of the Athenians and Spartans four or five centuries later? What but this, that every individual passes personally through a Grecian period. The Grecian state is the era of the bodily nature, the perfection of the senses, of the spiritual nature unfolded in strict unity with the body. In it existed those human forms which supplied sculptors with their models of Hercules, Phoebus, and Jove, not like the forms abounding in the streets of modern cities, wherein the face is a confused blur of features, but composed of incorrupt, sharply-defined, and symmetrical features, whose eye-sockets are so formed that it would be impossible for such eyes to squint and take furtive glances on this side and on that but they must turn the whole head. The manners of that period are plain and fierce. The reverence exhibited is for personal qualities, courage, address, self-command, justice, strength, swiftness, a loud voice, a broad chest. Luxury and elegance are not known. A sparse population and want make all people their own valet, cook, butcher, and soldier, and the habit of supplying their own needs educates the body to wonderful performances. Such are the Agamemnon and Diomed of Homer, and not far different is the picture Xenophon gives of himself and his compatriots in the *Retreat of the Ten Thousand*. "After the army had crossed the river Teleboas in Armenia, there fell much snow, and the troops lay miserably on the ground covered with it. But Xenophon arose naked and, taking an axe, began to split wood, whereupon others rose and did the like." Throughout his army exists a boundless liberty of speech. They quarrel for plunder, they wrangle with the generals on each new order, and Xenophon is as sharp-tongued as any, and sharper-tongued than most, and so gives as good as he gets. Who does not see that this is a gang of great people with such a code of honor and such lax discipline as great people have?

HOLMES: "Everything individuals see without them corresponds to their states of mind." We search in catacombs and libraries so that we may discover the self. We are the Greek, or else we could not understand them. We have already passed through the whole category of human experiences.

It these paragraphs, Emerson speaks of the "strict unity with the body." The spiritual nature referred to is the invisible prototype of the human form, having eyes that cannot squint and bodies shapely and symmetrical in form. These bodies the Greeks reveal in their sculpture.

EMERSON: The costly charm of the ancient tragedy, and indeed of all the old literature, is that the people speak simply. They speak as people who have great good sense without knowing it, before yet the reflective habit has become the predominant habit of the mind. Our admiration of the antique is not admiration of the old, but of the natural. The Greeks are not reflective, but perfect in their senses and in their health, with the finest physical organization in the world. They acted with the simplicity and grace of children. They made vases, tragedies, and statues such as healthy senses should, that is, in good taste. Such things have continued to be made in all ages and are now wherever a healthy physique exists. But as a class from their superior organization, they have surpassed all. They combine the energy of humanhood with the engaging unconsciousness of childhood. The attraction of these manners is that they belong to humankind and are known to everyone in virtue of all being once a child. Besides that, there are always individuals who retain these characteristics. A person of childlike genius and inborn energy is still a Greek and revives our love of the muse of Hellas. I admire the love of nature in the Philoctetes. In reading those fine apostrophes to sleep, to the stars, rocks, mountains, and waves, I feel time passing away as an ebbing sea. I feel the eternity of humankind, the identity of our thought. The Greeks had, it seems, the same neighbors as I. The sun and moon, water and fire, met their hearts precisely as they meet mine. Then the vaunted distinction between Greek and English, between Classic and Romantic schools, seems superficial and pedantic. When a thought of Plato becomes a thought to me, when a truth that fired the soul of Pindar fires mine, time is no more. When I feel that we two meet in a perception, that our two souls are tinged with the same hue and do, as it were, run into one, why should I measure degrees of latitude? Why should I count Egyptian years?

HOLMES: "Bard or hero cannot look down on the word or gesture of a child. It is as great as they," because the child acts instinctively from natural causes. It acts truly. Emerson was always searching for the instinctive act in the individual, the primordial genius, the original creative cause. His admiration was not for the antique, but for the natural. "A great child with good sense, it is Greek." The simplicity of naturalness draws the veil before the face of an antiquity, melting all times into one common eternity, into one universal identity of thought.

We measure time not in Egyptian years, but through the experience. The same incentive runs through the ages. Periods of time, destinies of nations, the achievement of individuals, the triumphs and defeats of societies all merge and find an outlet through every individual's mind, only to flow on into ages still unborn, into the eternal sea of never ending existence.

When we understand Plato, we can converse with him. When we understand the mind common to all individuals, language becomes universal. Time is not. All periods flow to one center that each one's soul individualizes.

EMERSON: Students interpret the age of chivalry by their own age of chivalry, and the days of maritime adventure and circumnavigation by quite parallel miniature experiences of their own. To the sacred history of the world, they have the same key. When the voice of a prophet out of the deeps of antiquity merely echoes to them a sentiment of their infancy, a prayer of their youth, they then pierce to the truth through all the confusion of tradition and the caricature of institutions.

Rare, extravagant spirits come by us at intervals, who disclose to us new facts in nature. I see that people of God have, from time to time, walked among humankind and made their commission felt in the heart and soul of the commonest hearer. Hence, evidently, the tripod, the priest, the priestess inspired by the divine afflatus.

Jesus astonishes and overpowers sensual people. They cannot unite him to history or reconcile him with themselves. As they come to revere their intuitions and aspire to live holily, their own piety explains every fact, every word.

HOLMES: "I see that people of God have always, from time to time, walked among humankind." All people are incarnations of the original Spirit, but some have penetrated more deeply into their own natures than others. These people "disclose to us new facts in nature." Those who reveal us inspire us. Those who discover themselves inspire the "soul of the commonest hearer." We cannot unite great souls like Jesus with the history of sensuality or materiality, because material history as a whole has not penetrated the same depth, has not dipped deeply into the infinite.

However, the infinite is still accessible through the finite, and the day comes in the evolution of our own consciousness when our "own piety explains every fact, every word" that Jesus uttered. The instinctive desire to worship or to commune with the true Spirit is alike in ancient and modern. As the mind penetrates spiritual causes, objective differences disappear, and the unity that remains unites Moses, Zoroaster, and Socrates with our own minds. They no longer belong to antiquity, and each person can say, "They are mine as much as theirs."

EMERSON: How easily these old worships of Moses, of Zoroaster, of Menu, of Socrates domesticate themselves in the mind. I cannot find any antiquity in them. They are mine as much as theirs.

I have seen the first monks and anchorets without crossing seas or centuries. More than once, some individual has appeared to me with such negligence of labor

and such commanding contemplation, a haughty benefi-
ciary begging in the name of God, as made good to the
nineteenth-century Simeon the Stylite, the Thebais, and
the first Capuchins.

The priestcraft of the East and West, of the Magian,
Brahmin, Druid and Inca is expounded in the individual's private life. The cramping influence of a hard
formalist on a young child in repressing its spirits and
courage, paralyzing the understanding, and that without
producing indignation, but only fear and obedience, and
even much sympathy with the tyranny, is a familiar fact
explained to the child when it becomes an adult, only
by seeing that the oppressor of its youth is itself a child
tyrannized over by those names and words and forms of
whose influence it was merely the organ to the youth.
The fact teaches it how Belus was worshipped and how
the Pyramids were built better than the discovery by
Champollion of the names of all the workers and the
cost of every tile. It finds Assyria and the Mounds of
Cholula at its door, and itself has laid the courses.

HOLMES: "The priestcraft of the East and West,
of the Magian, Brahmin, Druid, and Inca is expounded
in the individual's private life." Religion is a universal
sentiment. We are one with all its forms because we are
universal. There is neither east nor west for the soul. Our
own private life and inward emotions explain the passion and performance of every other person's life. The

religious emotion should not be stifled too much by the intellect.

The child finds itself tyrannized over by the "cramping influence of a hard formalist." The adult discovers that the formalist is itself tyrannized over by its own fears. The child has become an adult; the adult is still a child.

Through generations of misconception, we trace the cause of profane worship. Having traced this cause to its original source, the road leads again to our own door, to superstition, to fear and to misunderstanding, the foundation of which false structure is built on the cornerstone of dualism.

EMERSON: Again, in that protest which all considerate people make against the superstition of their times, they repeat, step for step, the part of old reformers and, in the search after truth, find like them new perils to virtue. They learn again what moral vigor is needed to supply the girdle of a superstition. A great licentiousness treads on the heels of a reformation. How many times in the history of the world have the Luthers of the day had to lament the decay of piety in their own households? "Doctor," said his wife to Martin Luther one day, "how is it that, whilst subject to papacy, we prayed so often and with such fervor, whilst now we pray with the utmost coldness and very seldom?"

HOLMES: "How many times in the history of the world have the Luthers of the day had to lament the decay of piety in their own households?" Luther illustrates every individual's life. The lips proclaim that which the heart does not feel, the intellect announces that which the soul rejects, and our everyday life too often contradicts our spiritual aspirations.

We are each complete when we strike a balance between our intellectual and spiritual qualities. We hedge ourselves around with misrepresentations, with superstitions and fears. Emerson's great theme is to lay bare the soul, loose the spirit, find the cause, be yourself. Live the life, and trust in the integrity of the universe.

EMERSON: Advancing individuals discover how deep a property they have in literature, in all fable as well as in all history. They find that the poet was no odd one who described strange and impossible situations, but that the universal ones wrote by their pens a confession true for one and true for all. Their own secret biographies they find in lines wonderfully intelligible to them, dotted down before they were born. One after another, they come up in their private adventures with every fable of Aesop, of Homer, of Hafiz, of Ariosto, of Chaucer, of Scott, and verify them with their own head and hands.

HOLMES: "Universal ones wrote by their pen a confession true for one and true for all." This refers to the generic person. It has a meaning identical with the Christ spoken of in the New Testament and, in modern metaphysical terminology, is referred to as the perfect or the God-intended person.

A great literature bears some relation to and in some way reveals this invisible presence, this spiritual completeness. When we looked deep into the soul, we have experiences that transcend mere intellectual deductions. From such inner communings follow our highest outward actions. The soul reveals wonders undreamed of by the intellect.

As the soul awakens, the intellect—human—"verifies them with its own head and hands." The inner impulse seeks to become objectified. The head and hands are instruments of the soul. The law of thought association and correspondences is always at work.

EMERSON: The beautiful fables of the Greeks, being proper creations of the imagination and not of the fancy, are universal verities. What a range of meanings and what perpetual pertinence has the story of Prometheus! Beside its primary value as the first chapter of the history of Europe (the mythology thinly veiling authentic facts, the invention of the mechanic arts, and the migration of colonies), it gives the history of religion with some closeness to the faith of later ages. Prometheus is the Jesus of the old mythology. He is the friend of humankind and stands between the unjust "justice" of the eternal Parent and the race of mortals, and readily suffers all things on their account. But where it departs from the Calvinistic Christianity and exhibits him as the defier of Jove, it represents a state of mind that readily appears wherever the doctrine of theism is taught in a crude, objective form, and which seems the self-defense of humankind against this untruth, namely, a discontent with the believed fact that a God exists and a feeling that the obligation of reverence is onerous. It would steal, if it could, the fire of God and live apart from God and independent of God. The Prometheus Vinctus is the romance of skepticism. Not less true to all time are the details of that stately apologue. Apollo kept the flocks of Admetus, said the poets. When the gods come among humans, they are not known. Jesus was not. Socrates and Shakespeare were not. Antaeus was suffocated by the grip of Hercules, but every time he touched the earth, his strength was renewed. Humankind is the broken giant, and in all our weakness, both our bodies and our minds are invigorated by habits of conversation with nature. The power of music, the power of poetry to unfix and, as it were, clap wings to solid nature interprets the riddle of Orpheus. The philosophical perception of identity through endless mutations of form makes us know the Proteus. What else am I who laughed or wept yesterday, who slept last night like a corpse and this morning stood and ran? And what see I on any side but the transmigrations of Proteus? I can symbolize my thought by using the name of any creature, of any fact, because every creature is human agent or patient. Tantalus is merely a name for you and me. *Tantalus* means the impossibility of drinking the waters of thought which are always gleaming and waving within sight of the soul. The transmigration of souls is no fable. I would it were. But human beings are only half human. Every animal of the barnyard, the field, and the forest, of the earth and of the waters that are under the earth, has contrived to get a footing and to leave the print of its features and form in some one or other of these upright, heaven-facing speakers. Ah! neighbor, stop the ebb of thy soul, ebbing downward into the forms into whose habits you have now for many years slid. As near and proper to us is also that old fable of the Sphinx who was said to sit in the roadside and put riddles to every passenger. If the passengers could not answer, the Sphinx swallowed them alive. If they could solve the riddle, the Sphinx was slain. What is our life but an endless flight of winged facts or events? In splendid variety, these changes come, all putting questions to the human spirit. Those people who cannot answer by a superior wisdom these facts or questions of time serve them. Facts encumber them, tyrannize over them, and make the people of routine the people of sense in whom a literal obedience to facts has extinguished every spark of that light by which humans are truly human. But if humans are true to their better instincts or sentiments and refuse the dominion of facts, as one that comes of a higher race remains fast by the soul and sees the principle, then the facts fall aptly and supple into their places. They know their master, and the meanest of them glorifies this master.

See in Goethe's *Helena* the same desire that every word should be a thing. These figures, he would say, these Chirons, Griffins, Phorkyas, Helen, and Leda are somewhat and do exert a specific influence on the mind. So far then are they eternal entities, as real today as in the first Olympiad. Much revolving them, he writes out freely his humor and gives them body to his own imagination. And although that poem is as vague and fantastic as a dream, yet is it much more attractive than the more regular dramatic pieces of the same author, for the reason that it operates a wonderful relief to the mind from the routine of customary images, awakens the reader's invention and fancy by the wild freedom of the design and by the unceasing succession of brisk shocks of surprise.

HOLMES: True imagination is not fanciful daydreaming. True imagination is fire from heaven. We must distinguish between the idle caprice of the mind and intuition, between reality and hallucination. Many fables were based on intuitive perceptions of truth and were prophetic. They foreknew and foresaw much that was to happen in the further evolution of the human race through the arts and sciences, government and religion.

The soul beholds these eternal truths in their unified beauty. The adoration of them is spontaneous, and worship becomes an interior communion rather than an external act. External worship is crude and mechanical; "reverence is onerous."

The fire of heaven is the candle of the Lord burning on the individual altar in the sanctuary of our own soul. It is never independent of the original flame. "Everyone is a divinity in disguise, a God playing the fool." Individuals are divine beings wearing a mask, largely unconscious of their own divinity, occasionally awakened by some flash of consciousness that temporarily reveals itself to the self and proclaims the eternal incarnation of a child begotten of the only God.

At such times, our language is divine and our music celestial. When the shroud of separation falls like a black mantle over our shoulders, our eyes become dimmed, our ears stopped, the heavenly music ceases, the vision vanishes, and, like a child crying in the night, we return to earth and separation. "They mope and wallow like dogs."

When great souls come among us, we fail to recognize them. Too often, our heavenly vision becomes suffocated by our external environment. The suggestion of separation and materiality smothers, but cannot quite extinguish, the divine spark. When we touch the original cause, our strength is renewed, the transcendent vision illuminates the consciousness, the harmony of celestial music unites us with the heavenly choir and has power to "clap wings to all solid nature." We see through the specific form and penetrate the universal identity—Proteus assuming any form he wills. From the essence of universal substance, any and all forms appear. We, too, have come up through all these forms, and though our faces are turned toward heaven, there is often a downward pull on the soul.

We must be careful to keep the vision clear. In the process of evolution, we have not yet entirely shaken off the weight of downward tendencies, "ebbing downward into the forms into whose habits you have not for many years slid."

One would infer that Emerson believed in an ascending gradation of consciousness. In this, he did not differ greatly from the theory of the modern evolutionist.

We are to keep our faces toward heaven because the central spark in the human is truly divine. The facts, forms, and events of human evolution are "winged." Each fact asks us who we are, and if we take the event too seriously, if the fact becomes too solid, if we "cannot answer by a superior wisdom, we are held in bondage." It is not by the fact or the form that we are held, but because the fact or the form temporarily extinguishes the true spark. We forget who we are and, hence, serve the fact and are held by the form.

When we see the Spirit in all facts and forms, everything falls into its logical place; everything glorifies the eternal unity. We master the fact, impersonate the form, both of which serve us. We have the power to transcend our environment and enter this hour into the full recognition of our true nature. We do this not by repudiating human existence, but by understanding it.

EMERSON: The universal nature, too strong for the petty nature of the bard, sits on his neck and writes through his hand, so that when he seems to vent a mere caprice and wild romance, the issue is an exact allegory. Hence, Plato said that "poets utter great and wise things which they do not themselves understand." All the fictions of the Middle Age explain themselves as a masked or frolic expression of that which in grave earnest the mind of that period toiled to achieve. Magic and all that is ascribed to it is a deep presentiment of the powers of science. The shoes of swiftness, the sword of sharpness, the power of subduing the elements, of using the secret virtues of minerals, of understanding the voices of birds, are the obscure efforts of the mind in a right direction. The preternatural prowess of the hero, the gift of perpetual youth and the like are alike the endeavor of the human spirit "to bend the shows of things to the desires of the mind."

In Perceforest and Amadis de Gaul, a garland and a rose bloom on the head of the one who is faithful and fade on the brow of the inconstant. In the story of the Child and the Mantle, even a mature reader may be surprised with a glow of virtuous pleasure at the triumph of the gentle Genelas, and indeed all the postulates of elfin annals—that the fairies do not like to be named; that their gifts are capricious and not to be trusted; that who seeks a treasure must not speak; and the like—I find true in Concord, however they might be in Cornwall or Bretagne.

Is it otherwise in the newest romance? I read *The Bride of Lammermoor.* Sir William Ashton is a mask for a vulgar temptation, Ravenswood Castle a fine name for proud poverty, and the foreign mission of state only a Bunyan disguise for honest industry. We may all shoot a wild bull, that would toss the good and beautiful, by fighting down the unjust and sensual. Lucy Ashton is another name for fidelity, which is always beautiful and always liable to calamity in this world.

HOLMES: "The universal nature, too strong for the petty nature of the bard, sits on his neck and writes through his hand." There is a power overshadowing us, an urge stronger than we are impelling us onward. This divine urge is not fully understood even by the most evolved. It sits on their necks and compels them to write.

Not fully understanding it and yet conscious of its subtle presence, they write extravagantly. Unable to understand its meaning, they are compelled to set down the symbol. The intuition transcends reason. The spiritual faculty announces; it does not argue. There is a heavenly language mingled with a babble of tongues. The "shoes of swiftness" bespeak the presence of the invisible Spirit. The garland of virtue fades on the brow of the unconstant. Truth alone rises triumphant. Its approach is silent. "Who seeks a treasure must not speak." It is to be found everywhere. Nature impersonates itself in countless forms. When we unmask nature, we behold the constant amid the complexity.

EMERSON: But along with the civil and metaphysical history of humankind, another history goes daily forward—that of the external world, in which they are not less strictly implicated. They are the compend of time; they are also the correlative of nature. Their power consists in the multitude of their affinities, in the fact that their lives are intertwined with the whole chain of organic and inorganic being. In old Rome, the public roads beginning at the Forum proceeded north, south, east, west to the center of every province of the empire, making each market town of Persia, Spain, and Britain pervious to the soldiers of the capital. So out of the human heart go, as it were, highways to the heart of every object in nature, to reduce it under the dominion of humankind. All individuals are bundles of relations, knots of roots, whose flower and fruitage is the world. Their faculties refer to natures out of them and predict the world they are to inhabit, as the fins of the fish foreshow that water exists or the wings of an eagle in the egg presuppose air. They cannot live without a world. Put Napoleon in an island prison, let his faculties find no people to act on, no Alps to climb, no stake to play for, and he would beat the air and appear stupid. Transport him to large countries, dense population, complex interests, and antagonist power, and you shall see that the individual Napoleon, bounded, that is, by such a profile and outline, is not the virtual Napoleon. This is but Talbot's shadow:

"His substance is not here:
For what you see is but the smallest part
And least proportion of humanity;
But were the whole frame here,
It is of such a spacious, lofty pitch,
Your roof were not sufficient to contain it."
                                        —*Henry VI*

Columbus needs a planet to shape his course upon. Newton and Laplace need myriads of ages and thick-strewn celestial areas. One may say a gravitating solar system is already prophesied in the nature of Newton's mind. Not less does the brain of Davy or of Gay-Lussac, from childhood exploring the affinities and repulsions of particles, anticipate the laws of organization. Does not the eye of the human embryo predict the light, and the ear of Handel predict the witchcraft of harmonic sound? Do not the constructive fingers of Watt, Fulton, Whittemore, and Arkwright predict the fusible, hard, and temperable texture of metals, the properties of stone, water, and wood? Do not the lovely attributes of the innocent child predict the refinements and decorations of civil society? Here also we are reminded of the action of human on human. A mind might ponder its thought for ages and not gain so much self-knowledge as the passion of love shall teach it in a day. Who knows themselves before they have been thrilled with indignation at an outrage or have heard an eloquent tongue or have shared the throb of thousands in a national exultation or alarm? No one can antedate their experience or guess what faculty or feeling a new object shall unlock any more than they can draw today the face of a person whom they shall see tomorrow for the first time.

HOLMES: "Out of the human heart go, as it were, highways to the heart of every object in nature." There is something in us akin to "the whole chain of organic and inorganic being." The greatest life is the one that includes the most. Inclusion, and not exclusion, is a helpful key to the philosophy of Emerson.

The objective world is the fruitage of the subjective.

"They cannot live without a world." Nature fits us for an objective existence. But we are not to think of this objective existence as being actually external. We are all truly united with it. The objective world is the fruitage of Spirit; it is rooted in pure cause. Spirit and matter are two ends of the same thing.

The individual must act. We must have a stake to play for. An unexpressed life is a fancy, a phantom, an empty dream. Cut us off from action, and we are lost. Being plays with becoming. The Spirit shapes itself into innumerable forms for the purpose of self-expression, self-recognition, and self-gratification. Our center is in being. The play of life upon itself goes on through us; the building blocks for the game consist of empires. Alps to climb, our science, our religions, our philosophies, all are playthings.

There is also the reaction of human to human, of thought to thought, of imagination to imagination, of emotion to emotion. The deep of nature and of the individual mind calls to the deep within us. We learn not by hearsay, not through theory, but by experience.

EMERSON: I will not now go behind the general statement to explore the reason of this correspondency. Let it suffice that in the light of these two facts—namely, that the mind is one, and that nature is its correlative—history is to be read and written.

HOLMES: When the depths of our nature are stirred, latent possibilities spring forth into accomplishment, and being passes forever fresh and new into a glorious becoming. There is something in us corresponding to everything we contact in life. From this viewpoint, "the mind is one; nature is its correlative; history is to be read and written."

EMERSON: Thus in all ways does the soul concentrate and reproduce its treasures for all students. They, too, shall pass through the whole cycle of experience. They shall collect into a focus the rays of nature. History no longer shall be a dull book. It shall walk incarnate in every just and wise person. You shall not tell me by languages and titles a catalogue of the volumes you have read. You shall make me feel what periods you have lived. All individuals shall be the Temple of Fame. They shall walk, as the poets have described that goddess, in a robe painted all over with wonderful events and experiences. Their own forms and features by their exalted intelligence shall be that variegated vest. I shall find in them the fore-world; in their childhood the Age of Gold; the Apples of Knowledge; the Argonautic Expedition; the calling of Abraham; the building of the Temple; the Advent of Christ; Dark Ages; the Revival of Letters; the Reformation; the discovery of new lands; the opening of new sciences and new regions in humankind. They shall be priests of Pan and bring with them into humble cottages the blessing of the morning stars and all the recorded benefits of heaven and earth.

HOLMES: "History shall no longer be a dull book. It shall walk incarnate in every just and wise person." The reference to the soul in this paragraph means the Universal Spirit or Over-soul. Emerson tells us that Spirit brings its entire being to all newborn humans. Everyone is the epitome of their being; they incarnate it. As they enter into it, it enters into them. The incarnation is not by proxy, not by hearsay or the reading of books, but through living.

We are each a microcosm containing within ourselves the same qualities, essences, and attributes of the microcosm. We are priest, saint, savior, and sinner. We are darkness and light, literature, law, and government. We are the interpreter of the universe, the ambassador of God, the one worshipping at the tomb, the Christ proclaiming its own divinity, the child at play, and the philosopher interrogating the universe. We are both question and answer, problem and solution, imagination, will, and purpose, fused into unity, manifest through variety, the light of the morning stars, and "all the recorded benefits of heaven and earth."

EMERSON: Is there somewhat overweening in this claim? Then I reject all I have written, because what is the use of pretending to know what we know not? But it is the fault of our rhetoric that we cannot strongly state one fact without seeming to belie some other. I hold our actual knowledge very cheap. Hear the rats in the wall, see the lizard on the fence, the fungus under foot, the lichen on the log. What do I know sympathetically or morally of either of these worlds of life? As old as the human race—perhaps older—these creatures have kept their counsel beside us, and there is no record of any word or sign that has passed from one to the other. What connection do the books show between the fifty or sixty chemical elements and the historical eras? Nay, what does history yet record of the metaphysical annals of humankind? What light does it shed on those mysteries which we hide under the names Death and Immortality? Yet every history should be written in a wisdom which divined the range of our affinities and looked at facts as symbols. I am ashamed to see what a shallow village tale our so-called history is. How many times we must say Rome and Paris and Constantinople? What does Rome know of rat and lizard? What are Olympiads and Consulates to these neighboring systems of being? Nay, what food or experience or succor have they for the Esquimaux seal hunters, for the Kanakas in their canoes, for the fishers, the stevedores, the porters?

Broader and deeper, we must write our annals—from an ethical reformation, from an influx of the ever new, ever sanative conscience—if we would more truly express our central and wide-related nature instead of this old chronology of selfishness and pride to which we have too long lent our eyes. Already that day exists for us, shines in on us at unawares, but the path of science and of letters is not the way into nature. The idiot, the primal, the child, and unschooled stand nearer to the light by which nature is to be read than the dissector or the antiquary.

HOLMES: The transcendent perception of Emerson's mind made him hold our slight knowledge rather cheaply. His mind encompassed a larger order than the average person is wont to envisage. The wisdom of antiquity, the morals of Confucius, the compassion of Jesus to him were not dead facts, but living presences. History was more than a record of human experiences; it was a revelation through the individual of the "one mind common to all individuals."

He spoke then from this larger viewpoint, this almost impersonal and yet personified viewpoint, when he said:

"I am the owner of the sphere,

of the seven stars and the solar year,

of Caesar's hand and Plato's brain,

of Lord Christ's heart and Shakespeare's strain."

The End

About the Authors

RALPH WALDO EMERSON (May 25, 1803–April 27, 1882) was born in Boston, Massachusetts. He attended Harvard College, graduating first in his class from Harvard Divinity School. In 1829, he was ordained at Boston's Second Church, where he also became chaplain to the Massachusetts legislature. Disagreements with the church's methods led to his resignation, after which he gradually moved away from theology and toward science. Later in life, he became a lecturer and began publishing his thoughts in a variety of essays which secured his place as one of America's great philosophers.

ERNEST SHURTLEFF HOLMES (1887–1960), an ordained Divine Science minister, was founder of a spiritual movement known as Religious Science, a part of the New Thought movement, whose spiritual philosophy is known as Science of Mind. He was the author of *The Science of Mind, How to Use Your Power,* and numerous other metaphysical books, as well as founder of *Science of Mind* magazine, in continuous publication since 1927.

Also from Newt List!

"How to" lessons on
relevant topics.

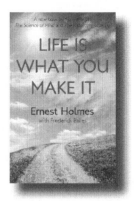

Ideas and techniques
for changing your life.

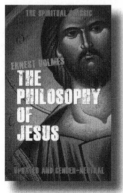

Understanding the life
and example of Jesus.

Interactive meditations
for greater mindfulness.

newt LIST

www.NewtList.com

Made in the USA
San Bernardino, CA
28 June 2016